THE GEFILTEFEST COOKBOOK

RECIPES FROM THE WORLD'S BEST-LOVED JEWISH COOKS

GRUB STREET · LONDON

Everyone eats. As a result, food is a wonderful way of connecting people. Recipes cut across all religious and national boundaries and *The Gefiltefest Cookbook* celebrates Jewish recipes from around the world.

Gefiltefest is a British Jewish food charity whose mission is to bring people together to explore the relationship between Judaism and food, educating and enthusing them about all aspects of Jewish food including food heritage, ethics, culture and traditions. Over a three-year period more than 65 chefs from around the world donated recipes to use in this, Gefiltefest's first cookbook. This edition includes an introduction by Gefiltefest's founding patron, Claudia Roden. It also contains a foreword by one of Gefiltefest's trustees, Maureen Kendler, with additional research by Claudia Prieto. For more information on Gefiltefest's work please visit www.gefiltefest.org.

Published in 2014 by
Grub Street
4 Rainham Close
London SW11 6SS
Email:food@grubstreet.co.uk
Web: www.grubstreet.co.uk
Twitter: @grub_street

Foreword © Claudia Roden, 2014
Introduction © Maureen Kendler, 2014
Recipes © Gefiltefest 2014
Copyright this edition © Grub Street 2014

Photography Michelle Garrett
Food styling Jayne Cross
Book Design Sarah Driver
Cover Design Sarah Baldwin

ISBN 978–1–909166–25–7

A CIP catalogue entry for this book is available from the British Library.

Printed in India

CONTENTS

INTRODUCTION

Gefiltefest is a Jewish food charity that aims to inspire people to change the way they think about food and to celebrate, promote and revive worldwide Jewish culinary traditions. A main event is an annual festival that takes place in London with talks, cooking demonstrations, food stalls and children's activities.

This engaging cookbook includes contributions from well-known Ashkenazi and Sephardi chefs and food writers from across the globe and also from people who just love to cook. It is appealing and so much more than a collection of recipes because it features personal favourites that you know are charged with emotion. And every recipe has a story behind it.

Food has always been of special importance to Jews. It is a link with the past and about roots and identity, ancestors and old homelands. Feasting is a major part of religious festivals and each festival has its own traditional dishes attached to it.

A major influence on the development of Jewish cooking has been the mobility of the Jews. Jews adopted the foods of the countries they lived in and adapted them to comply with their religious dietary laws. When they moved from one homeland to another it produced a fascinating interweaving of culinary traditions. Every Jewish community developed some distinctive dishes that were known as theirs.

My own community in Egypt was a mosaic of people from different parts of the Middle East, the old Ottoman Empire and North Africa, who settled in what was then a French-speaking cosmopolitan country. My family was originally from Aleppo in Syria and from Istanbul. When I look through the notes and recipes given to me by relatives and friends after we had all left Egypt, it rekindles, in a vivid way, nostalgic memories of a world which has long since vanished. When I cook my mother's dishes, make little filo packets, smell garlic sizzling with crushed coriander seeds, taste rose water in a milk pudding, I think of my parents holding hands as they always did when I went to see them in their house in Golders Green. I also remember the stories they kept retelling about their parents and grandparents and the people in our extended family.

I hope that you will enjoy reading, cooking and experimenting with the recipes that follow. I hope that you will be interested and inspired and that perhaps they may bring back for you treasured memories of loved ones and other now distant lands.

Claudia Roden
Founding Patron, Gefiltefest

FOREWORD

ON BEING REFINED, HEIMISCHE AND HYGIENIC
Early Jewish Cookery Books

Cookery books are so much more than a collection of recipes. They reflect the aspirations of their readers, how readers want their tables to look, how their kitchens should be organized and even how their families should behave. Arguably cookbooks tell us more about the wishes of a community than the actuality. Either way, Anglo-Jewish cookery books are an important record of both *what* we are and *who* we want to be. They may also tell us about the personal history of the author, along with his or her cultural background and their way of life.

For centuries, recipes were passed orally from generation to generation. No written records existed and women learnt to cook from their mothers and grandmothers. The advent of printing, however, meant that culinary knowledge slowly became available to anyone who could read.

Jewish cookery books have a special importance to Jewish communities because they are spread around the world. Waves of immigration in the nineteenth century resulted in the separation of countless families, and therefore there were difficulties in passing traditional recipes from generation to generation. Jewish cookery books were written for a newly-literate female readership, young women separated from an older generation who would have taught them what to cook and how. New cookbooks offered immigrants practical advice about which ingredients were available in their new homelands, together with reassurance in a time of great upheaval. Food is, after all, an emotionally laden and basic need.

The Anglo-Jewish cookery book story is unique. It reveals the differences between Jewish communities and the historical and social paths they follow in their adoptive countries. It also shows us that a distinctive Jewish cuisine did exist and that it is the result of the attempts to adapt to new countries and cultures.

The first Jewish cookery book to be published in England was in 1846, an intriguing volume written anonymously by 'a Lady'. This 'Lady' was, in fact, Judith, wife of Sir Moses Montefiore. The authorship of this book was an open secret, revealed only after her death in 1862, by Chief Rabbi Hermann Adler in his Yom Kippur sermon in which he paid fulsome tribute to Lady Judith's many achievements.

Judith was an outstanding woman in the community. Together with her husband, Sir Moses, their aristocratic status and role as leaders of the Jewish community was unquestioned. Her book was called *The Jewish Manual: Practical Information and Modern Cookery with a Collection of Valuable Hints Relating to the Toilette*. The recipes are a curious synthesis of Sephardic and Ashkenazi culinary traditions, which reflected the reality of the aristocratic households of the London Jewish community at the time, and the aspirations of the new immigrants. The cookery book also takes great pains to adjust non-kosher recipes for use in the kosher kitchen, and the message is clearly one in which Orthodox Judaism was to be adapted to the Gentile world and not remain cloistered in the ghetto.

The 'lard' problem – i.e. the replacing of lard with permitted substitutes – exercised Lady Montefiore considerably, as lard was ubiquitous in the English kitchen at the time. She establishes a tradition of ingenious substitutions of permitted foods for shellfish and pork in order to emulate the best of English cuisine. Thus the book offers mock-turtle soup and Cumberland pudding. The recipes are all strictly kosher, many being Dutch or Portuguese in origin, such as marinated fish and 'bola' cakes. There are a few nods to an international Jewish cuisine elsewhere, with German and Italian recipes, but there is a notable absence of any East European influence – the foods we might associate with Jewish cooking today, such as chopped liver and gefilte fish.

The book also reflects the fascination with all things French at the time, with recipes for *blanquette de veau* and *soupe de Cressy*. Even curried chicken makes an appearance. The nearest thing to an overtly 'Jewish' dish is a 'Luction pudding' which might be more familiar as a lokshen kugel. The author modifies this as 'Luction', also known as 'Rachel pudding'. This was possibly a dedication to Rachel D'Avigdor-Goldsmid, a newly arrived bride to her family.

The book offers advice to the family shochet, who would presumably accompany the reader on hunting and shooting expeditions, as to how to slaughter partridge and pheasant.

When this book was written – just before the tide of Ashkenazi immigration – the Jewish community was enjoying a period of relative stability. There were roughly 20,000-30,000 Jews in England, and the Jewish middle class was on the rise. A fine, kosher Victorian household run to the highest of standards was her vision here, and the book's price of five shillings, which would have been prohibitive for a poorer family, would have made it a serious investment. The book is directed at a female audience not worried by expense. Although the author advises against waste, expensive ingredients are called for, and it is assumed that the reader has servants to take care of domestic matters.

The book addresses itself to 'women of refinement' and introduces dishes 'in common use at refined English tables'. Without doubt, 'refined' was Lady Judith's favourite adjective. In the section on dress at the back of the book, she writes:

> '.... Simplicity should be preferred to magnificence; it is surely more gratifying
> to be admired for a refined taste, than for an elaborate and dazzling splendour;

'– the former always produces pleasing impressions, while the latter only provokes criticism.'

The Victorian ideal comports perfectly with Jewish notions of female modesty. Good taste and elegance is stressed throughout, with exhortations not to wear too much jewellery, to avoid extremes of fashion and any vulgarity. An underlying distaste and indeed fear of Jewish women being too showy and too attention seeking pervades the narrative. The table and those arranging it should aim to blend in to a cultured, albeit lard-free English society.

Estella Antrutel's *An Easy Economic Book of Jewish Cookery upon Strictly Orthodox Principles* (1880) with a dedication to Lionel de Rothschild, is rather more down to earth in its approach. It is aimed at 'beginners', reflecting a new readership, namely the thousands of poor Russian immigrants arriving. The author clearly understands the intense economic pressures of its readers, and urges them not to waste food. The content of this book would have been infinitely more useful, and indeed more comprehensible, to the newly arrived perplexed Eastern European family than Lady Judith's book, with its hints on how to keep a pleasingly pale complexion.

Antrutel's introduction stresses that keeping kosher is the most hygienic way to cook, stating that she has visited many Christian households where the meat is always salted, for health purposes. There is a defensive tone here, addressing the pressing need for hygiene in the kitchen, perhaps fearing that the new immigrants might abandon kashrut in their urge to assimilate into English society. In the wake of much anxiety about sanitation at this time in the overcrowded homes in London's East End, Antrutel's additional notes to the recipes pertain not so much to the ingredients, as to the importance of hygiene, working with clean hands, and washing vegetables thoroughly.

The pressures on newly arrived immigrants, where the men-folk were likely to be working long hours also concerned her, together with an assumption that even though women may also have been wage earners, providing the meals was entirely their responsibility:

> 'Wives should remember that good cooking will keep their husbands in good temper. It certainly must be very annoying to the husband that, having provided well for his table, he finds his wife does not take the trouble to see it is well cooked.'

The Economical Jewish Cookbook by May Henry and Edith Cohen (1897) applied the laws of kashrut to even simpler working class fare, with 'English' recipes for sausage rolls and roly-poly pudding. Henry may sensibly have decided to put the great middle class journey for the 150,000 Jewish families who arrived in this country after 1881 temporarily on hold. Yet a mere ten years on, May Henry's next book was entitled *Dainty Dinners and Dishes for Jewish Families*. Jews always considered the East End of London as a first and temporary stop, a holding place en route to the more desirable house and garden in the suburbs. The frequent reprints of *Dainty Dishes* over the next decades see a steady upmarket shift in tone. The word 'entrees' in the index together with recipes for dishes '*à la mode*' suggest that after ten years spent in London, and a consequently higher income, a degree more sophistication and 'daintiness' would have reached the strictly kosher table.

What the publication of these cookery books reveals to the modern reader is not only the way a British Jewish household ideally looked like and how women would have behaved, but also the beginning of the construction of an Anglo-Jewish identity. Contrary to America, as we will see later, this identity had roots in a profound respect for dietary laws, and, simultaneously a deep desire to assimilate into the local culture. The cookery books also show the concern of Jewish women of the time to conserve more orthodox traditions of Judaism without compromising the sophistication of their tables and parties. At the same time, they give us an insight into the backgrounds and origins of the Anglo-Jewish community.

In America a different community was forming. There were 250,000 Jews in the United States by 1880, and in fact their growing identity was to be often scornfully referred to as 'kitchen Judaism'. The main difference between British and American Jewish cookery books is the disregard for kashrut of the American community. As other traditional ties to the culture and ritual of the old world loosened, 'kosher-style' cookery and 'selectively treyf' eating became embedded in mainstream Jewish culture. Despite a more relaxed attitude to kosher ingredients the 'lard problem' also troubled American Jewish cooks, who eventually solved it with 'Crisco', a (rabinically endorsed) commercial vegetarian substitute. Crisco published a book for The Jewish Housewife in back to back Yiddish and English, encouraging the use of this 'modern' and 'digestible' fat, with the memorably modest tagline: 'The Hebrew race has been waiting 4,000 years for Crisco'.

Mrs. Esther Levy's *Jewish Cookery Book on Principles of Economy Adapted for Jewish Housekeepers with Medicinal Recipes and Other Valuable Information Relative to Housekeeping and Domestic Management* (Philadelphia: 1871) contains very few kosher recipes. Helpful and informative as its title suggests, this book does not aim to give those arrived in America airs and graces and a desire to do anything other than integrate quickly and efficiently.

One of the most popular American Jewish cookery books of all time, running to forty editions and selling nearly two million copies, the *Settlement Cookbook* calls for butter with meat, and includes shrimp and lobster. These reflect the Reform Movement from which these books emerged, as well as the more educated and ambitious women authoring them. This cookery book is a landmark in the American culture. It is also the most popular community cookery book of the history of the United States. It was compiled by Lizzie Black Kander, a Jewish homemaker, who gave cookery classes to poor girls and immigrants. Her objective was to show them how to assimilate in their new country, but also to give them the skills to be able to run the kitchens of Jewish households. The first edition of the book does contain Jewish traditional recipes, although they are sparse. Lizzie was sure the immigrants already knew how to cook gefilte fish, so she concentrated on more American recipes. In later editions the Jewish recipes disappeared completely.

As the *Settlement Cookbook* reveals, the Jewish community in America was willing to make important changes in its diet in order to assimilate in its new country. American Jews, on the whole, avoided pork in home cooking but enthusiastically ate ballpark hotdogs! Observance of kashrut with all its rules fell dramatically. Between 1914 and 1924 the consumption of kosher meat in New York fell by 30 per cent.

The rabbinate and other defenders of kashrut responded with a sponsorship of cookery books and pamphlets with titles such as *Yes, I Keep Kosher* and recommending kosher cooking as being both aesthetically desirable, and scientifically proven to be of superior nutritive value.

The rabbis and scientists who were producing the promotional material may have been male, but women wrote the cookery books which were used, inventing what was to be effectively a new genre of women's writing, one of great influence. Women such as 'Aunt Babette' (whose real name was Bertha Kramer) emerged as cultural authorities in their own right, promoted by publishers as balebostes, personifications of precious and precarious traditions. *Aunt Babette's Cook Book*, first published by Bloch Publishing Company in 1889 ran into dozens of editions. The book also encouraged a spirit of independence and creativity in the cook, something notably lacking in her English counterparts.

These books must have been a life raft to many young immigrant women, alone and far from home, anxious to recreate for themselves and their loved ones kitchens they had left behind them. The aspirational nature of the English books, with their admiration of all things upper class, whilst promoting conservatism and kashrut, contrasts with a bolder, 'kosher-style' melting pot American approach which would set the tone for community life on both sides of the Atlantic, in the century to come.

Maureen Kendler

STARTERS SOUPS SALADS LIGHT DISHES & DIPS

BORSCHT ON THE ROCKS

A chilled glass of that heart-of-the-winter favourite, beetroot borscht, makes a superb non-alcoholic aperitif for a spring or summer dairy lunch. If you prefer, you can serve a larger quantity in a soup cup as a cold starter for the meal – young beets give the borscht an amazing magenta colour, and teamed with a bowl of roses, it would create a delicious pink colour scheme for the table.

The calories can be trimmed by substituting Greek yoghurt or fromage frais for the more traditional soured cream, or use low-fat soured cream. Using a food processor to whisk the eggs and juice together is a good insurance against curdling. The beet juice can be frozen for 3 months, but once enriched with eggs and cream it's best to keep it refrigerated.

DAIRY OR PARVE / SERVES 6-8

3 bunches young beets (or 900g/2 lb old beets) • 1 medium onion
1 medium carrot • 1½ litres/6 cups hot water plus 3 vegetable stock cubes
15 grinds black pepper • 2 tablespoons sugar or granular substitute

To thicken
3 tablespoons lemon juice • 3 eggs
150ml/²/₃ cup soured cream, Greek yoghurt or creamy fromage frais

Have ready a 2 litre /2-quart soup pan. Trim the beets, wash thoroughly and peel only if old. Peel the onion and the carrot.

Cut all the vegetables into roughly 2½cm/1-inch chunks, then process in two batches until very finely chopped.

Put in the pan with the water, vegetables, pepper and sugar or sweetener. Bring to the boil, cover and simmer for 20 minutes, until the vegetables are soft and the liquid is a rich, dark red.

Pour the contents through a coarse strainer into a bowl and discard the vegetables. Return the strained beet juice to the pan and leave on a low heat.

Put the lemon juice and eggs into the food processor and process for 5 seconds, until well mixed.

With the motor running, pour two ladles of the hot beet juice through the feed tube and process for a further 3 seconds. Then add to the beet juice in the pan and heat gently, whisking constantly with a batter whisk or balloon whisk until the soup is steaming and has thickened slightly. Do not let it boil or it will curdle.

Taste and adjust the seasoning so that there is a gentle blend of sweet and sour.

Chill thoroughly. Just before serving, whisk in the cream, yoghurt or fromage frais.

NOTE

Cooked beet juice keeps 4 days under refrigeration, the complete soup for 2 days. Freeze 3 months. (Picture page 13)

ELIXIR OF FRESH PEAS

This pale green froth of a soup is the essence of fresh peas. Peas can travel in every flavour direction imaginable, but this soup needs nothing extra, although a few drops of truffle oil are intriguing. Plan to make it just before you serve it, unless you want to serve it chilled. The light, fragrant stock is made whilst you shuck the peas, and cooking time for the soup is about 4 minutes.

DAIRY /SERVES 4-6 AS A FIRST COURSE

1 bunch spring onions/scallions or 2 small leeks, including 5cm/2 inches of the
greens, thinly sliced • 5 large parsley stems, with leaves
Sea salt and freshly ground white pepper
700g/1½lb English pod peas, bright green and moist looking
1 teaspoon unsalted butter
75g/½ cup thinly sliced fresh onions or young leeks • ½ teaspoon sugar

Bring 1 litre/4 cups of water to a boil. As it's heating, add the spring onions, parsley, and ½ teaspoon salt. Add the peas as you shell them. Once the water comes to a boil, lower the heat. Simmer for 20 minutes, then strain.

Melt the butter in a soup pot and add the sliced onion. Cook over medium heat for about a minute, then add 125ml/½ cup of the stock so that the onions stew without browning. After 4 to 5 minutes, add the peas, another ¼ teaspoon salt and the sugar. Pour in 625ml/2 ½ cups of the stock, bring to a boil, and simmer for 3 minutes.

Transfer the soup to a blender. Drape a towel over the lid, and give a few short pulses to make sure it won't splatter. Then purée at high speed for 1 minute. Pour into small soup bowls and serve immediately.

Deborah Madison

MINESTRONE SOUP

This has always been a favourite with our family. A hearty soup might sound more for winter, but this is a lovely meal on its own, with crusty bread on a cool spring day. And, of course, for those with young families, a soup like this is a great way to get the children to eat vegetables!

I do hope you enjoy it.

PARVE /SERVES 6-8

2-3 tablespoons sunflower oil • 1 small onion, chopped finely
1 garlic clove, crushed • 1 celery stick, diced
2.25 litres/9 cups vegetable stock • 2 carrots • 1 medium potato, diced
1 teaspoon basil • 1 teaspoon oregano • ½ teaspoon salt
¼ teaspoon pepper • 400g/14oz tin chopped tomatoes in tomato juice
120g/¾ cup mini macaroni pasta

Slowly fry the onion in oil in a large saucepan until soft and golden. Add garlic and celery to soften.

Add carrots, potato and herbs and let them sweat. Add stock and simmer for 1 hour. Add more water if necessary.

Add chopped tomatoes and simmer for 20 minutes and stir in pasta 10 minutes before serving. Enjoy!

Lady Sacks

LENTIL SOUP

This soup can be traced all the way back to the Old Testament. In Genesis 25:29-34 you can read how Jacob's brother, Esau, sold his birthright as oldest son to his younger brother, merely for a bowl of Lentil Soup! So yes, this soup is truly delicious and comforting. Whether you should sell your birthright for it? Well, I will let you decide on that.

MEATY /SERVES 6-8

For the soup

2 tablespoons olive oil • 1 onion, finely chopped
2 sticks celery, finely chopped • 1 large carrot, finely diced
1 leek, white part only, cleaned and finely chopped
350g/1½ cups brown lentils, washed and drained
2 litres/8 cups Beef, Chicken or Vegetable stock
Juice of 1 lime • 1 teaspoon ground cumin
1 teaspoon salt • ¼ teaspoon black pepper

For garnish

6 slices old bread • olive oil to drizzle over the croutons
1 tablespoon olive oil • 2 onions, sliced in rings
½ teaspoon mild curry powder • garlic or garlic salt

For the soup heat the olive oil on a medium heat. Add the finely chopped onions and gently fry without colouring for 10 minutes or until softened.

Then add the celery, carrot and leek, again gently fry without colouring. Add the lentils, mix all ingredients gently and pour in the stock. Bring to the boil and once boiling reduce the heat, simmer covered for at least 2 hours, stirring occasionally.

When lentils are soft, stir in the cumin, lime, salt and pepper.

While the soup is simmering, preheat the oven to 180°C/350°F/gas 4. Slice each bread slice into cubes and sprinkle with olive oil and if you like, garlic or garlic salt.

Place on a baking sheet and bake for approximately 15 minutes or until cubes are dried. Keep an eye on them to make sure they don't burn.

When you are about to serve the soup, fry the onions in olive oil and season with curry powder.

Pour the ready soup into a serving dish, add the fried onions, croutons and enjoy!

Claire Berson

CHICKEN SOUP WITH HANDMADE EGG NOODLES

There's no soup in the world like my grandmother's chicken soup. As it cooks, it fills the whole house with an intoxicating holiday aroma. My grandmother's freezer always holds big bags full of the soup and we enjoy it at every meal, winter or summer, holiday or not. The homemade noodles are so simple to prepare, even tastier than croutons and healthier too. I use chicken wings to prepare the soup because they have lots of taste hidden away in them.

MEATY /SERVES 8-10

5 celery stalks with leaves • ½ bunch dill • ½ bunch parsley
10 chicken wings • 4 chicken drumsticks • 1 turkey neck • 1 parsley root
1 small white onion • 4 carrots • 5 small red potatoes • 1 kohlrabi
Salt, freshly ground pepper

Handmade Egg Noodles
240g/½ cup potato flour • 240g/½ cup water • 6 eggs, beaten
Salt, pepper • Oil for frying

Place the greens (celery, dill and parsley) at the bottom of a large pot. Wash the wings, the drumsticks and the turkey neck well in cold water and lay them on the greens.

Peel the parsley root, onion, carrots, potatoes and kohlrabi and lay them on top of the poultry parts.

Cover ingredients with mineral water or filtered water and bring to a boil. Lower the flame, add salt and pepper and cook over a low fire for 1 to 1½ hours.

Michal Ansky

HANDMADE EGG NOODLES

Mix the flour and water in a medium-sized bowl. Add the beaten eggs and season with salt and pepper. Mix to a smooth batter.

Heat a small amount of oil in a frying pan/skillet. Pour a thin layer of the batter into the pan, creating a kind of very slender pancake; fry until golden on both sides.

Place a few of the pancakes on top of one another and roll them up into a plump log. Slowly slice the log into thin strips (less than 1cm/½-inch wide). Serve with the soup.

NOTE

This recipe is suitable for Passover and is especially useful for gluten-sensitive diners. For a delicate anise flavour, add 1 tablespoon of chopped tarragon to the batter. The noodle logs can be kept frozen and used as needed.

WARM SHAV WITH SALMON KREPLACH

After winters of eating stodgy, stored and pickled vegetables, Russian and Polish Jews welcomed spring by making cold tart lemony sorrel soups including shav and botvinya.

Reading about botvinya which combines sorrel, spinach and pieces of fish, I thought about the salmon and creamy sorrel sauces of the Loire. Rough chunks seemed too indelicate so I encased the salmon in wonton wrapper kreplach.

DAIRY /SERVES 6-8

Kreplach
2 spring onions/scallions, thinly sliced • 30g/1oz unsalted butter
350g/¾lb fresh salmon, skinned, boned and cut into chunks
1 large egg yolk • 2 tablespoons snipped fresh chives • Salt and pepper
36–40 wonton wrappers (have a few extra in case of tearing)
Melted butter

Shav
125g/1 cup finely chopped onion • 30g/1oz unsalted butter
400g/8½ cups (tightly packed) sorrel, washed, stemmed and cut into thin strips
475ml/2 cups cold water, preferably bottled
475ml/2 cups milk or 1 cup milk and 1 cup heavy or light cream
2 tablespoons snipped fresh dill • Salt and pepper • 2 large egg yolks
250ml/1 cup sour cream

Prepare the kreplach by cooking the spring onions in butter in a medium frying pan over moderately low heat, stirring until softened. Add the salmon and continue cooking for 4 to 5 minutes, gently tossing the mixture, until the fish is barely cooked through.

Let cool slightly, then stir in the egg yolk, chives, salt and pepper to taste.

Process the mixture in a food processor, pulsing until fine.

Transfer the filling to a bowl, cover and refrigerate for 1 hour or until cold.

Jayne Cohen

Mound a heaped teaspoon of the filling in the centre of a wonton wrapper. Dipping your finger in water, moisten the wonton wrapper all around the filling. Fold the wrapper over to make a triangle and with your fingers press out all the air around the filling. Press the edges very firmly together to form a tight seal and press down the edges with the tines of a fork.

Continue making the kreplach until all the filling has been used up, folding each one into a neat triangle.

Bring at least 5 litres/5 quarts of lightly salted water to boil in a large, wide pot. Slip in the kreplach, one by one, being careful not to overcrowd the pot. Lower the temperature slightly and poach until tender, 3 to 6 minutes depending on the brand of wonton wrapper. Remove a few at a time with a large slotted spoon, allowing any excess water to drain back into the pot. Gloss the kreplach with a little melted butter and set aside.

Prepare the soup by cooking the onions in the butter in a large saucepan over moderately low heat for about 10 minutes until very soft. Stir in 375g/8 cups of the sorrel, turn the heat up to medium and cook for 5 to 7 minutes until it has melted into a purée.

Add the water, bring the mixture to a boil and simmer for 10 minutes. Add the milk (and cream if you are using it), dill, salt and pepper to taste and heat slowly until the soup is hot. Do not let the soup come to a boil.

In a bowl, whisk the egg yolks with the sour cream. Slowly pour a cup of the hot soup into the egg-sour cream mixture, stirring to prevent curdling. Gradually stir this mixture back into the soup and cook whilst stirring over a low heat for 3 or 4 minutes to blend the flavours. If you prefer a smoother soup, you can purée the soup in a blender at this stage.

Stir in the reserved 25g/½ cup sorrel strips.

NOTES

To serve, place 5 or 6 kreplach in each shallow soup plate and ladle the warm shav over them. Garnish with chopped spring onions, dill and a small dollop of sour cream.

Accompany the shav with dark rye or pumpernickel bread, butter and a sauvignon blanc.

SALATIT BANJAN – SMOKY EGGPLANT SALAD WITH GARLIC AND PARSLEY

The eggplant (aubergine) has been known as a suspect vegetable in some cultures. According to the food scholar Charles Perry, the Greek *melitzana* and Italian *melanzana* come from the Latin *mala insana*, meaning 'mad apple'. In the same vein, the Sanskrit name *vatingana*, from which the Arabic finds its source, means 'belonging to the windy class', a designation associated with madness. Egyptians have a saying when someone contradicts himself: '*Adi zaman al-batinjan*', or 'it's eggplant time'. But Arabs and Jews have always embraced this curious vegetable. As early as the 7th century, Arabs ate eggplant and called it *sayyid al-khudar*, 'the lord of the vegetables'. The scorn historically lodged against eggplant may come from the difficulty of rendering it fit to eat; indeed, the foam-like pulp must be cooked well to be eaten. Here, the eggplant is cooked over direct fire. The charred flavour that this method imparts is essential to this recipe. Oven roasting simply does not produce the distinctive smokiness that contrasts wonderfully with the earthy tomato and acidic lemon in this salad.

PARVE /SERVES 4-6

2 medium eggplants (aubergines) • 1 medium tomato, chopped
1 green bell pepper, seeded and chopped (optional)
5 tablespoons chopped flat leaf parsley • Freshly squeezed lemon juice (to taste)
1 tablespoon extra virgin olive oil
3 garlic cloves, chopped (about 1½ teaspoons) • 1 teaspoon ground cumin
½ teaspoon Aleppo pepper or ¼ teaspoon crushed red pepper
1 teaspoon kosher salt/ground sea salt

Pierce the skins of the eggplants in a few places with a fork. Place each eggplant directly into a medium-high gas flame. The skins of the eggplants should eventually blister and shrivel. Remove eggplants from heat once they are thoroughly charred and you can sense that the flesh inside has become heavy with moisture. It may take about 30 minutes to arrive at this point. Let cool.

Cut eggplants vertically in half and scoop out their flesh, placing it into a colander. Discard the peels. Press the eggplant flesh firmly against the colander to remove excess liquid.

In a medium bowl combine eggplant flesh with tomato, green pepper, parsley, lemon juice, oil, garlic, cumin, pepper, and salt. Give it a good stir.

CRUNCHY LOKSHEN CABBAGE SALAD

Rather than reserving lokshen for a stodgy winter pudding or hot chicken soup, try serving this salad which is quick to make, sweet, sour, crunchy and a brilliant way of using up a small amount of lokshen.

PARVE / SERVES 10

1kg/2 lb white cabbage shredded • 100g/3½oz thin vermicelli

Dressing
25ml/1oz sesame oil • 75ml/2½oz orange juice
2 tablespoons runny honey • ½ teaspoon ginger purée
½ teaspoon lemon juice • Salt and black pepper

Shred white cabbage.

In a frying pan, dry fry vermicelli until golden brown.

Mix dressing ingredients together.

Incorporate all ingredients.

Add salt and black pepper to taste.

SWEETHEART SALAD

A slightly tart dressing complements the sweet ingredients in this salad. It's named after my sweetheart sister-in-law who shared this recipe with me.

PARVE /SERVES 4-5

Salad
1 head romaine lettuce, chopped • 250ml/1 cup pineapple, fresh, cubed
50g/¼ cup dried apricots, chopped • 50g/¼ cup dried cranberries
50g/¼ cup roasted almonds • 1 green apple

Dressing
3 tablespoons lemon juice • 2 tablespoons oil
¼ teaspoon salt • 1 tablespoon sugar

In a large bowl, combine lettuce, pineapple, apricots, cranberries, and almonds.
Combine dressing ingredients.
Right before serving, core and slice the apple, with peel on, add to salad, and toss with dressing.

Leah Shapira

AVOCADO AND ARUGULA SALAD WITH TOMATOES AND CUCUMBERS

Avocado adds a luscious flavour and texture to this Israeli-style chopped salad. Choose avocado that is ripe but not too soft so you can dice it. With such a rich addition, you may find you don't need to add any oil. This salad is a lovely accompaniment for broiled or grilled salmon, roasted chicken or grilled meat. On an appetizer platter, it's great with smoked salmon or even with gefilte fish.

PARVE /SERVES 4

4 medium tomatoes, diced small
½ to ⅔ hothouse cucumber or small, slim tender cucumbers
(about 225g/½lb), diced small
30g/1 cup coarsely chopped arugula (rocket)
30g/1 cup shredded romaine lettuce or bok choy leaves
1 or 2 ripe avocados, preferably Haas • Salt and freshly ground pepper
1 tablespoon freshly squeezed lemon juice (optional)
1 tablespoon extra virgin olive oil (optional)

Combine tomatoes, cucumber, arugula and romaine in a bowl and toss lightly.

Just before serving, halve avocado, remove peel and scoop out flesh. Dice the flesh, add to salad and toss lightly.

Sprinkle with salt and pepper and toss again. Add lemon juice and olive oil if you like. Serve as soon as possible.

Faye Levy

ARUGULA SALAD WITH DATES AND CHÉVRE

Vanilla is generally associated with desserts, not salads. However, the subtle sweetness this extract brings to the dressing really complements the salad ingredients.

DAIRY /SERVES 4-6

120g/4oz arugula • 8 large, pitted, soft Medjool dates
30g/¼ cup diced red onion • 115g/4oz crumbled goat cheese (see Note)
30g/¼ cup dry-roasted, shelled sunflower seeds
60ml/¼ cup pomegranate vanilla vinaigrette (see below)

For the Pomegranate Vanilla Vinaigrette
120ml/½ cup extra virgin olive oil • 60ml/¼ cup unseasoned rice wine vinegar
60ml/¼ cup pomegranate molasses (available in Middle Eastern markets)
2 teaspoons sugar or 1 teaspoon honey • 1 teaspoon vanilla extract
Salt and freshly ground pepper to taste

To make the Pomegranate Vanilla Vinaigrette combine all of the ingredients in a screw-top jar. Shake until well blended.

Rinse the arugula and pat dry with paper towels. Place in a salad bowl. Lightly oil a cutting knife and cut the dates in half lengthwise. Cut each half crosswise about 2 or 3 times. Set aside.

Toss the arugula with 60ml /¼ cup of the dressing. Place on 4 or 5 individual plates. (Or alternatively toss everything together in one large bowl and serve).

Evenly distribute the dates, onion, crumbled goat cheese, and sunflower seeds on each plate. Grind a little black pepper on top, and drizzle with the remaining dressing.

NOTE
½cm/¼-inch-thick rounds of goat cheese whose edges are rolled in cracked pepper may be added to individual salads as an alternative to the crumbled goat cheese.

If you are presetting your salad plate on the dinner table for a party, reserve the chopped onion in a dish in the refrigerator, and sprinkle on at the last minute to avoid having the room filled with the scent of onions.

Medjool dates are the large, soft date variety that are easily cut or mashed into a paste if needed. Try to avoid packets of chopped dates as they are heavily coated with sugar to prevent sticking.

Tina Wasserman

ARABIAN OLIVES

I call these olives 'Arabian' because the spices represent the Moors' influence on the Spanish palate through the introduction of Middle Eastern spices to Iberian cuisine.

PARVE /SERVES 1

100g/4oz pitted green olives, drained • ¼ teaspoon ground cumin
¼ teaspoon dried oregano
¼ teaspoon lightly crushed dried rosemary leaves • ¼ teaspoon dried thyme
1 bay leaf • ¼ teaspoon fennel seed • 2 cloves garlic, lightly crushed
2 tablespoons sherry vinegar • 1 teaspoon grated lemon zest

Place the drained olives in a clean glass jar that is just large enough to hold the olives and the remaining ingredients with 2.5cm/1 inch of headroom. Use a jar just slightly larger than the one the olives came in so that the olives can be covered with a minimum amount of liquid and lessen the amount of air in the jar.

Add the remaining ingredients to the jar, and fill the jar with water just to cover all of the olives. Shake well and marinate at room temperature for 2 days.

Store indefinitely in refrigerator.

ABC SALAD – ASPARAGUS, BILTONG AND CROUTONS

If it's different textures you love then this salad is for you. The flavours of this salad are enhanced by the young, fresh, spring herbs, whilst the crunch of the croutons and crispness of the water chestnuts seem to work so well with the plump firmness of the tomatoes.

MEATY /SERVES 4-6

250g/10oz fresh green asparagus, cut into 1cm/½-inch slices
250g/10oz broccoli stems, cut into 1cm/½-inch slices
250g/10oz cherry tomatoes, cut in half • 1 can water chestnuts, finely sliced
1 large red onion, roughly chopped
35g/1oz basil/flat leaf parsley, roughly chopped
55-70g/2-2½oz finely shredded biltong (Beef Jerky) (If biltong isn't available you
can use about 100g/3½oz smoked steak, finely shredded and fried in a little oil
until crispy. Remove from heat and allow to cool before sprinkling over salad)
60g/2 cups health bread croutons (see recipe below)

Salad Dressing
120ml/½ cup red wine vinegar • 235ml/1 cup olive oil
2 tablespoons brown treacle sugar • ½ teaspoon mustard powder
1 teaspoon crushed fresh garlic • 1 teaspoon salt
1 teaspoon crushed black pepper

Sharon Lurie

CROUTONS

Remove crusts and cube 1 loaf of your favourite health bread.

Spread the cubes out on a baking sheet. Spray with olive oil spray and sprinkle with garlic and herb spice.

Bake on 150°C/300°F/gas 2 until golden brown.

SALAD

Whisk the dressing ingredients together.

Place sliced broccoli into bowl, pour boiling water to cover and allow to steep for 1 minute.

Drain boiling water off and immediately place into cold water.

Do the same with the asparagus but leave them to steep for less time, about 15 to 20 seconds.

Place asparagus and broccoli into a large salad bowl, add tomatoes, sliced water chestnuts, onion and basil or parsley.

About 1 hour before serving, pour salad dressing over vegetables and toss lightly.

Refrigerate.

Just before serving, toss salad again. Add croutons and biltong and toss again so that croutons absorb some salad dressing, but still remain crunchy.

MOROCCAN ORANGE AND OLIVE SALAD

Jews were the cultivators of the orange groves throughout the Mediterranean region. The Moors brought the bitter oranges (similar in taste to a blood orange) to Cordoba and the south of Spain. From there, the taste for oranges migrated south to Morocco.

PARVE /SERVES 4-6

4-5 large blood or navel oranges • 2 tablespoons fresh lemon juice
3 tablespoons walnut oil • 2 cloves garlic, finely minced • Salt to taste
60g/¼ cup Arabian olives (see Tina Wasserman recipe on page 29)
Chopped fresh mint or paprika for garnish (optional)

Slice off the tops and bottoms of the oranges.

Using a sharp knife, slice off the peel and the pith from the oranges following the natural curve of the fruit.

Cut each orange horizontally into ½cm/¼-inch thick slices. Cut each slice into quarters and place in a bowl.

Combine the lemon juice, walnut oil, garlic, and salt in a screw-top jar and shake to combine. Add more lemon juice or salt if needed.

Toss some of the vinaigrette with the oranges, and then add the olives and toss.

Place salad on a plate, and garnish with some mint or a sprinkling of paprika if desired.

NOTE

The best way to tell if a citrus fruit has a good flavour is to scratch the peel with your fingernail. Even if the fruit is tart, the scent should be sweet and full-bodied; a lemon will smell like a lemon lollipop if good.

It is better to add dressing to citrus fruit at the last minute; otherwise the dressing will macerate the fruit or pull the juices out of the fruit.

Tina Wasserman

SPRING ASPARAGUS AND PICKLED RED ONION SALAD

This is an excellent starter for a Shabbat or holiday dinner. There is just something so elegant about asparagus stalks, with their bright green colour and tight, floral-like tips. Asparagus is one of the vegetables that really signals the coming of spring and that our winter dependence on root vegetables is coming to an end.

DAIRY/SERVES 6

Asparagus
36 jumbo asparagus spears, peeled
200g/2 cups Pickled Red Onions (see recipe below)
225g/3 cups mixed baby salad • 250ml/1cup sherry vinegar
and mustard vinaigrette • Parmesan cheese

Pickled Red Onions / makes about 2½ cups
2 red onions • 500ml/2 cups water • 500ml/2 cups red wine vinegar
225g/1 cup sugar • 1 teaspoon salt • ½ teaspoon ground black pepper
¼ teaspoon mustard seeds • ¼ teaspoon coriander seeds • 1 bay leaf

To make the Pickled Red Onions thinly slice the onions.

Combine the water, red wine vinegar, sugar, salt and pepper in a saucepan, bring to simmering over medium heat, stirring to dissolve the sugar.

Wrap the seeds and bay leaf in a small piece of cheesecloth, tying closed with kitchen twine. Add this spice sachet and the onions to the saucepan and bring to boiling.

Immediately remove the pan from the heat and let the onions reach room temperature in the pickling liquid.

Discard the spice sachet and if not ready to use the onions, transfer them and the liquid to a container and refrigerate for up to 3 weeks.

Bring a medium saucepan of lightly salted water to simmering over high heat, add the asparagus and boil until al dente – 3 to 4 minutes.

Using tongs, transfer the asparagus to a bowl of ice water and allow to chill completely. Transfer the asparagus to kitchen towels to drain. (Recipe continues on page 36)

Todd Gray and Ellen Kassoff Gray

Lay 6 asparagus spears on each of six plates and divide the pickled red onions equally over the asparagus.

In a large bowl, toss the salad greens with the vinaigrette to taste and mound them on top of the onions and asparagus.

Shave very thin slices of Parmesan cheese and lay them over the salad.

Drizzle with additional vinaigrette if desired.

CHICORY AND FRISÉE SALAD WITH BLUE CHEESE, CROUTONS AND PECANS

An excellent starter (appetizer) salad, or to serve after a fish or dairy main course.

DAIRY /SERVES 8

125ml/½ cup extra virgin olive oil • 2 fat cloves garlic, finely sliced
4 thick slices bread, cut in 1cm /½-inch cubes • 50g/½ cup pecan halves
2 packs frisée • 6 small heads of chicory (Belgian endive), cut lengthwise into 4
75g/½ cup crumbled Stilton or similar blue cheese

Dressing
3 tablespoons fresh lemon juice • 3 teaspoons white wine vinegar
½ teaspoon each salt and caster sugar • 10 grinds of black pepper

Flavour the olive oil with the garlic by leaving them together for 2 hours, then strain out the garlic.

Arrange the bread cubes in a shallow ovenproof tray (baking pan), drizzle them with 3 scant tablespoons of the oil and season with a little salt.

Toss well to coat evenly, then bake for 15-18 minutes at 190°C/375°F/gas 5, until golden brown.

Put the pecan halves in a small baking tin, then crisp at the same time as the bread cubes (check colour half-way through). Allow to cool.

To make the dressing, put the lemon juice and vinegar together with the remaining garlic oil, the salt, sugar and black pepper into a screw-top jar. Shake until slightly thickened.

An hour before serving, combine the frisée, chicory, pecans and cheese in a large bowl. Shortly before serving, add the dressing and toss until all the ingredients are evenly coated. Turn salad into a salad bowl and scatter with the croutons.

Evelyn Rose

SPRING SALAD OF NEW POTATOES, YELLOW SQUASH, PEAS, HERBS AND GOAT'S CHEESE

This is such a delicious and fresh salad for the tiny potatoes which are just making their appearance in the spring. The peas, herbs, goat's cheese and first of the season's tiny yellow squash continue the celebration — if yellow squash is not available, the salad is delicious without it. Ditto if all three colours of potato are not available; delicious with any tiny new potatoes of spring.

DAIRY /SERVES 4-6

650-700g/1½lb tiny new potatoes, washed and whole • 1 yellow zucchini (courgette) or similar summer squash, cut into large dice
About 75g/2½oz sugar snap peas • ½-1 clove garlic, finely chopped
About 4 tablespoons fresh spring peas (I use frozen, straight from the freezer)
2-3 tablespoons extra virgin olive oil, or as desired
About 2 teaspoons wine vinegar, or as desired
About 3 tablespoons fresh tarragon leaves, whole or coarsely chopped
Handful chives, coarsely chopped • Salt and pepper to taste
Approx 150g/5oz soft white goat's cheese

Boil the potatoes in their skins until just tender. Drain and cool.

When cool enough, peel off the skins then cut them into bite-sized pieces/chunks. If using different coloured potatoes, the darker colours, such as the blue or pink, will leech their colour onto the paler, creamy spuds. Therefore it is helpful to cook them separately or in batches, starting with the paler potatoes first, then lifting them from the hot water and adding the darker ones.

Steam or blanch the yellow zucchini and sugar snap peas briefly. Set aside.

Toss potato chunks with the zucchini, sugar snap peas, and garlic, then gently mix in the peas, olive oil, vinegar, tarragon, and chives. Season with salt and pepper.

Serve topped with the goat's cheese, either in dollops or crumbled, depending on how soft and creamy the cheese is.

Eat right away, or chill for later.

Marlena Spieler

SPRING BATTER FRIED BABY ARTICHOKES WITH GARLIC ROUILLE

Contrary to what one might expect, baby artichokes are not immature, nor even a special variety. They grow right on the same plant with larger artichokes. Nonetheless, they are much easier to eat and this delicate crunchy batter makes them a perfect dish for a light spring menu.

DAIRY /SERVES 6

250g/2 cups all-purpose (plain) flour • 355ml/1½ cups of pale ale
A pinch of ground marjoram
1 kg/2 lb baby artichokes, small, green and tightly closed, trimmed
1 teaspoon salt • 700ml/3 cups peanut oil
Grated Parmigiano-Reggiano, to taste

Dipping sauce
1 clove garlic • Pinch salt
1 egg yolk • 240ml/1 cup of extra virgin olive oil
A few drops lemon juice

Make a simple beer batter by combining the flour and beer. Stir until smooth and add a pinch of marjoram.

Cut off the bottom stem of each baby artichoke, remove some of the outer leaves and cut each in half. Remove any fuzzy hairs from the interior. Submerge the baby artichoke halves immediately into batter as you trim them.

Heat a pot with the peanut oil to 180°C/350°F. Carefully place a few batter-covered artichokes into the oil one at a time without crowding.

When golden brown remove them to a cooling rack or a paper towel lined plate and lightly dust with salt.

Sprinkle with grated cheese whilst still hot. Repeat until all artichokes are fried.

TO MAKE THE SAUCE

Pound the garlic with a pinch of salt in a mortar, add the egg yolk and continue pounding until smooth.

Add the oil drop by drop and continue to pound until thick.

Add a few drops of lemon juice. Serve with the fried baby artichokes.

Ken Albala

TABOULEH – COUSCOUS VEGETABLE SALAD

The Lebanese claim that we stole this recipe directly from their culinary heritage, and honestly, there might be a seed of truth in that claim. But whereas the Lebanese tabouleh is a relatively simple (however, no less tasty) combination of bulgar wheat and chopped fresh herbs, the Israeli version is much richer – a sort of fruit and vegetable extravaganza, enriched with pine nuts and pomegranate seeds. And since we Israelis are not as hard working as the Lebanese, our tabouleh is based on instant couscous, found in your local supermarket.

PARVE /SERVES 10

1 bag instant couscous • 4 tomatoes • 4 cucumbers
4 spring onions /scallions • 2 lemons • 6 tablespoons olive oil
3 tablespoons kosher salt or ground sea salt
1 tablespoon freshly ground black pepper
30g/½ cup pine nuts, lightly toasted
150g/1 cup pomegranate seeds (or dried cranberries)
20g/½ cup chopped coriander • 20g/½ cup chopped parsley
20g/½ cup chopped dill

Prepare instant couscous and let it cool down completely.

Finely dice the tomatoes and cucumbers. Thinly slice the scallions and mix together with the other vegetables.

Add zest from one whole lemon and juice from both lemons to the salad.

Add the rest of the ingredients, including cold couscous, to the salad and mix well. This salad keeps well in the fridge for up to 24 hours.

Gil Hovav

KASHKARIKAS AND KALAVASUCHO

Turkish Jews have kept alive a food culture that is greatly influenced by their Spanish heritage as well as traditional Turkish cuisine. Jewish cuisine in Turkey has been passed from mother to daughter and features recipes which as well as representing the comfort of home and the value of traditions, makes clever use of simple ingredients and creative use of leftovers. This recipe is just one such example: creating two delicious dishes from one vegetable, using both the peel and the flesh. This recipe is a tribute to my grandmother and to all the Jewish women who have given us, through cooking, the gift of love.

KASHKARIKAS KON AVRAMILA – COURGETTE PEEL IN OLIVE OIL AND PLUM GREEN SAUCE

PARVE /SERVES 8

2kg/4lb medium-size courgettes
½ kg/1lb sour green plums, stones removed or juice of two lemons
120ml/½ cup extra virgin olive oil • 240ml/1 cup water
Dill, finely chopped • 1 tablespoon sugar
Salt and freshly ground black pepper

With a knife peel the courgettes lengthwise in strips leaving some of the flesh still on the peel. Cut the peel crosswise into 3cm /1¼-inch slices and set aside the flesh for the recipe below.

Boil the plums in the water, strain and crush them.

Combine the plum juice (or lemon juice), olive oil, sugar, salt and pepper in a saucepan. Bring to a boil and then reduce the heat to medium and cook for 5 minutes. Add the courgette peel, cover and simmer for about 10 minutes or until cooked al dente. The liquid should have reduced to a syrupy consistency.

Sprinkle with dill and let it cool in the pan, covered.

Serve at room temperature.

Sibel Cuniman-Pinto

KALAVASUCHO – COURGETTE GRATIN WITH FETA AND KASHKAVAL CHEESE

DAIRY /SERVES 8

2 kg/4lb courgette flesh
4 slices bread, crusts removed, soaked in water and squeezed dry
6 large eggs • 120ml/½ cup olive oil • 250g/8oz feta cheese
250g/8oz grated kashkaval or manchego cheese
Dill, finely chopped • Mint, finely chopped
Flat leaf parsley, finely chopped • Salt and freshly ground black pepper

Preheat the oven to 180°C/350°F/gas 4.

Grate the courgette flesh, allow to drain for 20 minutes, squeeze dry to remove all the liquid and transfer to a large bowl.

Add the bread, eggs, oil, cheeses, fresh herbs, salt and pepper to the courgettes and mix well.

Brush a baking dish with oil, pour in the mixture and top with more grated cheese.

Bake for 30–40 minutes until golden.

NOTE

Serve with a green salad and a yoghurt, cucumber and garlic sauce. Both courgette dishes marry well with a fruity rosé wine.

CUCUMBER ROLLS WITH SOFT GOAT'S CHEESE

This is my modern take on the Middle Eastern salad of cucumber, yoghurt and garlic. Traditionally, it is served as a dip or as an accompaniment to grilled fish or meat. I wanted to prepare a pleasing starter for our lunch, one fine spring day. And these cucumber rolls filled with a spicy, soft cheese did the trick. Light and refreshing, it is a definite favourite with my husband and our friends.

DAIRY / SERVES 2

1 cucumber (small Mediterranean one, if possible)
100g/3½oz very soft goat's cheese or cream cheese
Extra virgin olive oil, to mix • Salt and cayenne pepper, to taste
½ clove garlic, very finely chopped or crushed
1 fresh tomato, diced (for garnish) • Pinch of za'atar herb or dried thyme

Wash the cucumber. Do not peel.

With a potato peeler, slice the cucumber length-wise into paper-thin strips and lay them flat on a chopping board.

Mix the soft cheese with two tablespoons of olive oil or more to make a smooth paste. Add the cayenne pepper, the salt and the garlic and mix well.

Put a teaspoon of the mixture at one end of each cucumber strip and roll carefully to the end. Do this with as many strips as you need.

To prepare individual servings, drizzle a little olive oil on each plate and arrange upright with four or five rolls per person. Decorate with the chopped tomato and sprinkle liberally with za'atar. You can drizzle on more olive oil if you wish.

Serve with warm pitta bread.

NOTE

Variation: Make one cucumber roll per person. Put two tablespoons of yoghurt in the middle of each individual plate. Pour two tablespoons of olive oil over it. Season. Stand the roll in the middle of the yoghurt. Arrange a few cucumber slices all around the plate and decorate with the chopped tomatoes. Sprinkle generously with za'atar.

Linda Dangoor

M'FARKA – SPINACH IN SCRAMBLED EGGS

Served with hot baked flatbreads, this is one of the many Babylonian Jewish specialities that we used to eat for breakfast in Baghdad. Apart from spinach, we have other egg dishes where mincemeat or salted goat's cheese is mixed with egg to produce small fritters or a tortilla style cake. These were mainly served for breakfast. The steamed spinach and scrambled eggs make a delicious combination. I love to cook it today for lunch or a light dinner. It is nutritious and so easy to rustle up. I use spring baby spinach because of its delicate texture and flavour. You can use mature spinach leaves, of course, but don't forget to remove the middle stalks and to shred the leaves.

PARVE /SERVES 2

1 small or medium onion, finely chopped
100g/3½oz baby spinach, washed and drained • 2 eggs, lightly beaten
1 tablespoon sunflower oil • Salt and pepper to taste

Heat the oil and sauté the onions until soft and golden.

Throw in the spinach and stir-fry until it becomes very limp and the water has evaporated. Add a little salt and pepper.

Pour in the beaten eggs and keep stirring to mix. Cook for about five minutes or until the eggs are cooked but still soft and fluffy. Season lightly again.

NOTE

Serve hot or cold with some warm pitta bread.

Linda Dangoor

LEEKS AND FENNEL IN ANISE VINAIGRETTE

The classic French 'poireaux vinaigrettes' have always appealed to me as a first course. The poached leeks marinated in a tangy dressing are elegant and appetite-whetting at the start of a meal. But, it occurred to me that the recipe could take on a different personality if fennel bulbs were combined with the leeks. I also added anise seed and tarragon to the dressing to reinforce the liquorice delicacy of the fennel.

PARVE /SERVES 4

4 medium-size leeks, trimmed and well-rinsed
1 large fennel bulb, rinsed, stems removed • 2 litres/8 cups water
125ml/½ cup tarragon vinegar • Salt
1 garlic clove • Leaves from 6 sprigs fresh tarragon
1 teaspoon anise seed • 60ml/¼ cup extra virgin olive oil

Cut leeks down so as to leave only an inch of green. Slice about ½cm/¼-inch from the bottom of the fennel bulb. Slice vertically in 4 sections, each about 2.5cm/1-inch thick.

Select a non-reactive pan large enough to hold leeks and fennel in a single layer, add water, half the vinegar and a generous pinch of salt. Add leeks and fennel, bring to a simmer, cover and poach gently for 15 to 20 minutes, until the vegetables are tender. Remove leeks and fennel from pan, draining well, and set on several layers of paper towel for 10 minutes, turning them once, to fully drain.

Using a small food processor, a spice grinder or mortar, grind the garlic, tarragon leaves and anise seed together. Mix with remaining vinegar. Beat in olive oil. Season with salt.

Arrange leeks and fennel in a serving dish. Beat dressing again and pour over vegetables. Allow to marinate for at least 1 hour at room temperature before serving.

Serve as a first course or as part of an hors d'oeuvre or salad buffet. The leeks and fennel are also lovely to serve alongside cold chicken or fish. The dish is perfectly parve. Sauvignon blanc is the wine of choice.

Florence Fabricant

COTTAGE CHEESE PANCAKES

This is a wonderful Shavuot dish, but in our house, my mother made the pancakes for Sunday brunch and on birthdays. Serve them with soured cream and jam, and fresh fruit salad on the side – very Russian Empire. They're best warm, but I've been known to snack on the cold leftovers, straight from the fridge, with a blessing, of course.

DAIRY /SERVES 4

4 eggs • 110g/½ cup sugar • 450g/1 lb cottage cheese
60g/½ cup flour • 2 tablespoons soured cream • Pinch of salt
Pinch of baking powder • Butter for frying

Beat eggs and sugar together in a metal mixing bowl. Add remaining ingredients and stir well.

Melt butter in a large frying pan. Spoon the batter into the pan, making 10cm/4-inch pancakes. Flip when browned. Some people like them crispy; others prefer them golden. If the pancakes fall apart whilst cooking, add more flour and sugar to the batter.

Remove cooked pancakes and keep warm in a covered dish in a low oven. Continue frying until all the batter is finished.

Sue Fishkoff

COLD SPRING ROLLS

My Spring Roll is a close relative of the conventional Chinese egg roll, except that it is not deep fried, is served at room temperature and at only about 120 calories, is surprisingly filling.

You can fill the paper wrap with virtually any shredded or julienned vegetable or fruit. Sliced chicken, beef, seared tuna or salmon can also be added but I typically make mine parve and fill the wraps with smoked or baked tofu.

PARVE /SERVES 4

25g/1oz thin rice noodles • 4 x (20cm/8 inch) rice paper rounds
50g/½ cup shredded cabbage and/or lettuce • 10g/¼ cup fresh mint
10g/¼ cup fresh coriander (cilantro) • 10g/¼ cup shredded carrot
4 pieces baked tofu (optional)

Cover the noodles with hot water and soak for 15 minutes, then drain well and pat dry with paper towels.

Fill a shallow pan or plate large enough to accommodate the rice paper round with warm water. Soak one rice paper in the water until it just starts to become pliable – about 30 seconds. Transfer to a work surface and place on top of a paper towel.

Arrange the lettuce or cabbage and the rest of the ingredients on the bottom half of the rice paper round, leaving a 2.5cm/1inch border along the edge. Roll up the rice paper tightly around the filling, fold in the sides and continue rolling. Transfer to a plate and cover with dampened paper towels.

Repeat with the rest of the rice paper wrappers.

Serve the rolls halved on the diagonal with your favourite dipping sauce.

If you plan to serve them fresh, you can put some sauce inside the roll. If you plan to serve them the next day, remove the rolls from the fridge an hour before serving.

Tamar Genger

ASPARAGUS AND NEW POTATOES

Locally-grown English asparagus is only around for a month or so in May. It has an exquisite taste – quite different from the imported spears available all year round. Hot asparagus needs only melted butter but to make it into a more substantial starter, I add Jersey Royals and serve it cold. My mother *always* peeled these tiny new potatoes – for the look and the taste – so I do too. But unlike her, I cook the asparagus in the microwave – a brilliant improvement. Home-made mayonnaise is the finishing touch, but you could use Hellman's. Fresh mint adds that extra English springtime flavour.

PARVE /SERVES 4
450g/1lb fresh English asparagus
450g/1lb Jersey Royal new potatoes (very small), peeled
2-3 sprigs fresh mint leaves
4-6 tablespoons home-made or bought mayonnaise • Juice ½ lemon
Salt, pepper

Cut the ends off the washed asparagus and trim the pale ends with a potato peeler to remove the tough outer skin.

Arrange the asparagus in a shallow dish, sprinkle over a few tablespoons of salted water, cover and microwave for about 6 minutes on full power. (You need very little water with this method.) Leave to stand for a minute and then drain and refresh with cold water.

Cook the peeled new potatoes for 8-10 minutes in salted water with a sprig of mint. Test to see if they are tender, then drain and cool. Arrange the asparagus and potatoes on a large serving dish or individual plates.

Stir a little lemon juice into the mayonnaise and drizzle it over the potatoes. Add more fresh mint to garnish.

NOTE
Serving idea: To make the dish into a main course you could add some flakes of freshly poached salmon or smoked mackerel.

Judy Jackson

SPINACI CON PINOLI E PASSERINE – SAUTÉ SPINACH WITH PINE NUTS AND RAISINS

This is a traditional Roman Jewish dish which I grew up with and is well known within the Jewish community in Rome, but otherwise relatively unknown. It is easy and delicious and can be served on toasted bread as bruschetta or as a side dish to accompany either fish or meat. It is often served for Shabbat or High Holidays.

PARVE /SERVES 4-5

1 kg/2.2lb fresh spinach leaves • 4-5 tablespoons extra virgin olive oil
1 onion, finely chopped • Handful raisins • Handful pine nuts
Salt and freshly ground black pepper, to taste

Wash the spinach well and without draining it, put it in a deep saucepan, cover and leave it to steam with a tablespoon of rock salt for 5-7 minutes.

You don't need to add any additional water when steaming the spinach as it releases its own liquid whilst cooking. By not adding water, the spinach also retains all of its precious vitamins.

Once the spinach is tender, drain it, leave it to cool down and squeeze the water out.

In the meantime, heat up the olive oil and the chopped onion in a non-stick frying pan with some salt and pepper. Leave to cook, stirring occasionally, for 5 minutes until the onion is soft and starts to turn golden. Add the steamed and squeezed spinach; stir to blend in the oil and onion and leave to cook for 8-10 minutes.

Soak the raisins in a little cold water for a minute so they become soft and juicy. Squeeze them and add them to the spinach together with the pine nuts. Stir well and leave to sauté for another 5 minutes.

Serve warm and enjoy!

Silvia Nacamulli

PURIM SPICED RAISIN AND DATE CHALLAH

This glorious recipe is based on the super rich challah recipe from my book and every time I make this challah with my lovely daughter Sarah I'm so proud that I am passing on such a precious heritage and legacy to her family. By adding dried fruit and spice this recipe becomes almost a fruit bread and perfectly suitable for Purim when our thoughts turn to celebration and enjoyment. Any left-over challah is delicious toasted with butter or turned into pain perdu.

If you prefer, you could halve the amount of dried fruit and spice and make half the dough plain and the other half with fruit and spice.

PARVE /MAKES 4 LARGE LOAVES OR 40 BULKIES

385ml/1½ cups warm soya milk

2 generous pinches ground saffron (about ⅛ teaspoon)

2 tablespoons active dried yeast • 1 tablespoon Fairtrade soft brown sugar

1 tablespoon honey • 1 tablespoon corn or golden syrup

1kg + 100g/8½ cups organic strong white bread flour – the best you can buy

3 teaspoons salt

5 organic free-range eggs plus 2 egg yolks for the mixture
and 1 egg yolk for glazing

115ml/½ cup light olive oil, plus extra for greasing

200g/1 cup raisins soaked in 2 tablespoons orange juice (or Kiddush wine)

200g/1 cup chopped dates

2 teaspoons ground cinnamon or mixed spice

Poppy seeds, sesame seeds or even hundreds and thousands, to decorate

Ruth Joseph

In a small bowl, combine 240ml /1 cup of warm water with the warm milk, saffron, yeast, sugar, honey, golden syrup and 100g of the flour.

Whisk until smooth and no yeast lumps remain. Set aside in a warm place to ferment for about 20 minutes until the mixture is bubbling (I put the bowl on the hob above my lit oven).

In a large bowl, combine the remaining flour with the salt (I use my mixer with the dough hook attached).

Beat together the eggs and egg yolks, add to the yeast mixture, pour in the oil and beat with a fork until smooth.

Pour the wet ingredients into the flour bowl and mix to a soft, pliable dough. You may need to add a little more oil or flour, depending on the dryness/wetness of the mixture. Knead the mixture by hand for 10 minutes or by machine for 6-8 minutes.

Place the dough in a large, clean, oiled bowl.

Cover with a cloth or oiled cling film and leave to rise in a warm place for 40-60 minutes or until doubled in size. Alternatively, leave to rise overnight in the fridge, which definitely improves the flavour.

Preheat the oven to 200°C/400°F/gas 6 and line 2 baking sheets with baking parchment.

Tip the risen dough out onto a floured work surface, knock out the air with your fists and mix the dried fruit and spice into the dough.

Shape into plaits or individual bulkies.

Place on your prepared baking trays, cover with a clean cloth or oiled cling film and set aside to prove in a warm place for 30-40 minutes until doubled in size.

Make an egg wash by beating together the remaining egg yolk with a little oil and glaze the challahs all over. Sprinkle with seeds and bake in the hot oven for about 30-35 minutes until golden. Bulkies will take about 20 minutes. You will know when they are cooked because they will sound hollow when you tap them on the base.

ÛS E SPARCS – EGGS AND WHITE ASPARAGUS AS CONSUMED IN FRIULI-VENEZIA GIULIA

Eggs and white asparagus are harbingers of spring eagerly embraced in Friuli-Venezia Giulia, the region in north-eastern Italy that has one of Europe's largest synagogues in Trieste, the capital city. As the seaport of the Austro-Hungarian Empire and a region that has been influenced equally by Vienna and Venice, 'FVG' has an historic Jewish community that also includes members from Greece. It has sensational wine, especially whites. This delicious dish can be a starter or a main course. Be sure to use the freshest ingredients possible, as that is what makes it most tasty.

PARVE

Hard-boiled eggs (1 per person as an appetizer; 2 per person as a main course)
1 kg/2lb fresh white asparagus (plan on 4-5 stalks per person as a starter; 8-10 as a main course)
Excellent quality wine vinegar (white or traditional balsamic are best)
Extra virgin olive oil • Salt and freshly ground black pepper

Make hard-boiled eggs (see the instructions on page 56 for tips). Once they are ready, remove the shells. Now it is time to cook the asparagus.

Peel the bottom third of each asparagus stalk and cut off the base if it is tough.

Boil the asparagus upright in lots of water (do not cover the tips with water) or steam them laying them down in a pan in a little water. When you can stab the thickest part of a stalk with a fork, it is ready.

Place 4 or 5 stalks on each plate for a starter. For a main course, place 8 to 10 stalks on each plate.

Fred Plotkin

Place 1 egg (for starters) or 2 eggs (for main courses) on each plate. Cut each egg in half lengthwise before serving.

Present the plates to diners and pass the vinegar and oil at the table, as well as the salt and pepper mill. The most traditional way to eat this is for each diner to mash the eggs with the tines of a fork and then pour on some vinegar and a few drops of oil. The dominant taste should be vinegar, whilst the oil should serve to make the combination smoother. Add a little salt and pepper and stir so that an egg sauce is created that can be slathered on the asparagus or used as a dip.

NOTE

Some people do not mash the egg, but simply cut it in larger pieces and add vinegar and oil and small amounts of salt and pepper. They scoop this up with a piece of asparagus. I encourage you to try the classic method.

The perfect grape wine to pair with eggs and/or asparagus (green or white) is Sauvignon blanc. Ideally, it should come from Friuli-Venezia Giulia or elsewhere in north-eastern Italy, but you may also use Sauvignon blancs from Styria (Austria) or France.

HARD-BOILED EGGS

Everyday foods we take for granted are the ones that require the most care to prepare successfully. These are tips to making hard-boiled (or hard-cooked) eggs special.

Select the freshest eggs possible. In many so-called developed countries, eggs are sold refrigerated. In other advanced nations, including Italy, they are often sold at about 20°C/68°F and at home will sometimes be refrigerated and sometimes not. If you purchase refrigerated eggs in a carton, be sure to keep them refrigerated until you need them.

To hard-boil, take a medium-size saucepan made of glass, enamel or stainless steel and gently place the eggs in the pan. There should be enough room for the eggs to move about easily. Add enough cold water to the pan so that the eggs are entirely covered but ensure that the water will not bubble out when boiling.

Bring the water to a boil over medium heat, with the pot uncovered. Then lower the heat to a simmer, cover, and cook the eggs for another 10 minutes. If the eggs you are using were cold from the refrigerator, cook the eggs for 12 minutes rather than 10. Once the eggs are cooked, immediately place them in cold water (I use ice in the water). This will prevent further cooking and discolouration of the yolks. If you intend to eat the egg hot, then remove it from the water. Otherwise, let it cool in the water.

To shell a hard-boiled egg, gently tap one end against a hard surface. Then roll the egg in the palms of your hands for a couple of moments This will loosen the shell, which should be relatively easy to pull off if you start at the point at which you made a crack.

Fred Plotkin

FARFALLE WITH PEPPERS AND BASIL

The combination of peppers, sun-dried tomatoes, basil and vinegar makes for a light, colourful and delicious dish which is equally good served warm or at room temperature.

PARVE /SERVES 4–6

1 yellow bell pepper • 1 red bell pepper
5 sun-dried tomatoes, packed in oil • 4 tablespoons extra virgin olive oil
2 cloves garlic, minced • Kosher salt • 450g/1lb farfalle
40g/1 cup tightly packed fresh basil leaves, torn into small pieces
1-2 tablespoons balsamic vinegar • Freshly ground black pepper

Preheat the grill. Set the rack in the grill pan and cover it with foil.

Cut the peppers in half lengthwise, core and seed them.

Make a shallow basket with a piece of heavy duty foil, crimping in the corners so that the liquids do not spill out.

Set the foil basket on the grill rack and arrange the peppers inside, skin side up.

Place the grill pan under the grill as high up in the oven as possible and grill for about 7 minutes until the skin is blistered and charred.

Remove the peppers from the grill, cover with foil and allow to cool.

Peel the peppers and cut them into small cubes.

Cut the sun-dried tomatoes into small cubes.

Heat the olive oil in a large saucepan, add the garlic and sauté for a few seconds over a low heat. Add the peppers and tomatoes and sauté for another minute.

Cook the farfalle in boiling salted water until al dente and drain well in a colander.

Add the farfalle to the sauce and combine. Add the basil and toss. Season to taste with the vinegar, salt and pepper.

Helen Nash

GRILLED MACKEREL ON TOASTED SOURDOUGH WITH SALSA VERDE AND PICKLED CUCUMBER

This dish is perfect for eating al fresco. Enjoy these sandwiches on one of those first spring afternoons when the warm sun finally breaks through after a long winter. Although these are essentially glorified sandwiches, they are full-on flavour: chilli, garlic, lime, salty capers, cooling cucumber, all brought together by some tasty grilled mackerel and a dollop of mayonnaise. Perfect!

PARVE /SERVES 4

1 cucumber, peeled • 6 tablespoons white wine vinegar • 2 teaspoons sugar
Large pinch of salt • 1 mild red chilli, finely chopped
4 very fresh mackerel, filleted • Extra virgin oil
8 slices of white sourdough bread • 4 tablespoons mayonnaise
Fresh rocket

Salsa Verde
6 tablespoons flat leaf parsley, very finely chopped
4 tablespoons rinsed capers, very finely chopped
8 tablespoons extra virgin olive oil • Juice of 1 lime
1 clove garlic, crushed • Large pinch of salt

Using a peeler, peel ribbons from the cucumber, turning it as you go to get ribbons of an equal width. Once you reach the seeds at the centre, discard this part.

Mix the vinegar with the sugar, salt and chopped chilli. Drop in the cucumber ribbons and marinate for 10 minutes before draining.

Mix together the salsa verde ingredients.

Preheat a grill to its highest setting.

Season the fish with salt and black pepper and rub with olive oil.

When the grill is hot, place the fillets, skin side up, on a lightly greased tray and grill for 4 minutes until the skin is crisp and the flesh is cooked. Remove from the grill.

Lightly toast the bread, spread mayonnaise on 4 of the slices and lay 2 fish fillets on each. Spoon over the salsa verde and then top each off with some drained cucumber. Cover with some rocket and the remaining slices of toast.

Alan Rosenthal

TUNISIAN COUSCOUS WITH FENNEL, RED PEPPERS AND GARLIC

Of the numerous North African couscous recipes I've come across since writing *Couscous and Other Good Food from Morocco*, this red and green Tunisian speciality is one of my favourites. The mélange of dill and fennel, celery leaves, red pepper flakes, and spices makes for a light and delicious couscous. In winter, in Tunisia, large fennel bulbs produce 45cm/18-inch stalks, bearing bushy bunches of thin fern-like greens. You may have tried fennel tops and found they have little taste, but when you use a hefty amount of these greens you will discover that they have flavour and can contribute real earthiness to a dish. There are numerous variations on this recipe. In the city of Sfax, they make it with malthouth, or grilled and cracked barley grits, instead of couscous grains. I have also tasted it when made with whole wheat couscous. But the best version is this recipe which uses ordinary store-bought couscous. The recipe was given to me by Aziza ben Tanfous, curator of the Sidi Zitouni Museum on the island of Jerba, who learned it from her grandmother on the mainland.

Since this type of couscous tends to be slightly dry, you may want to serve it with glasses of buttermilk, the traditional way.

PARVE / SERVES 6

20g/½ cup dill and fennel (anise) leaves • 20g/½ cup parsley
Handful celery leaves • Handful carrot tops
75g/½ cup spring onions/scallions and leeks • 125ml/½ cup olive oil
150g/1 cup chopped onion • 3 tablespoons tomato paste
2 tablespoons crushed garlic • 2 teaspoons sweet paprika
2 teaspoons salt, or more to taste • 2 teaspoons ground coriander or tabil
1 teaspoon ground caraway
1½-2 teaspoons dried red pepper flakes, preferably Aleppo, Turkish
or Near East pepper for best flavour
450g/2½ cups medium grain couscous
1 fresh green chilli, stemmed, seeded and minced
1 red bell pepper, stemmed, seeded, and cut into 6 parts
6 garlic cloves, peeled and left whole

Paula Wolfert

Wash the herbs and leaves under running water. Drain and roughly chop. Wash and chop the scallions/spring onions and leeks. Fill the bottom of a couscous cooker with water and bring to a boil. Fasten on the perforated top; add greens, scallions and leeks and steam, covered, for 30 minutes. Remove from the heat and allow to cool, uncovered. When cool enough to handle, squeeze out the excess moisture and set aside.

Heat the olive oil in a 25cm or 30cm/10- or 12-inch skillet (frying pan) and add the onion. Cook 2 to 3 minutes to soften, then add the tomato paste and cook, stirring, until the paste glistens. Add the crushed garlic, paprika, salt, coriander or tabil, caraway and red pepper flakes and cook slowly until the mixture is well blended. Add 250ml/1 cup water, cover, and cook for 15 minutes.

Remove the skillet from the heat. Stir the dry couscous into the contents of the skillet and stir until well blended. Stir in the steamed greens, leeks and scallions and mix well. Fold in the green chilli, red pepper and garlic cloves. Fill the bottom of the couscous cooker with water and bring to a boil. Fasten on the perforated top, add the contents of the skillet, and steam, covered, for 30 minutes.

Turn out the couscous onto a large, warm serving dish. Use a long fork to break up lumps; fish out the whole garlic cloves and red pepper slices, reserving them. Stir 250ml/1 cup water into the couscous, taste for seasoning, and cover with foil. Set it in a warm place for 10 minutes before serving.

Decorate the couscous with the red pepper slices in a star pattern and place the whole garlic cloves on top. Serve with glasses of buttermilk.

ONION AND GOAT'S CHEESE TART

I have fond memories of this tart, which my mother – who is an amazing cook – used to make for weekend lunches when we were younger. It also reminds me of summers in the South of France as the goat's cheese and caramelised onion combination is classically French. Olives, sun-dried tomatoes and anchovies all make good additions to the topping.

Whenever she served it we noshed it up in minutes. No wonder, as it looks and tastes delicious. It is quick and easy to make – even more so if you keep a bag of caramelised onions in the freezer ready to defrost. Make a double quantity of the onions, so you can use half and freeze the other.

DAIRY/SERVES 6

2 tablespoons olive oil • 450g/1lb/3½ cups onions, sliced
1 level tablespoon caster sugar • 225g/2 cups self-raising flour
1 level teaspoon baking powder
25g/1½ tablespoons butter, chilled and cubed
25g/2¼ tablespoons Parmesan cheese, grated
150ml/¼ pint milk, room temperature • 100g/½ cup goat's cheese, crumbled
1 or 2 sprigs of fresh thyme, leaves picked

Preheat the oven to 190°C/170°C (fan)/ 375°F/gas 5. Line a baking sheet with baking parchment.

Heat the olive oil and add the onions. Turn the heat down low and cover the pan. Cook for about 10 minutes until they are soft.

Sprinkle them with the sugar and season with salt and pepper and turn the heat up to medium. Cook for another 5-10 minutes until they are caramelised. They should be soft but not browned and all moisture should have evaporated.

Whilst you are softening the onions, sift the flour and baking powder.

Rub in the butter and stir in the grated Parmesan.

Measure the milk and set aside.

Mix the milk into dry ingredients and mix to a soft dough.

Roll out the dough into a circle about 1cm/½-inch thick and prick with a fork. Put on the baking sheet and arrange the onions and goat's cheese on top. Sprinkle with the thyme and bake until golden brown – approximately 20 minutes.

Serve warm or at room temperature.

Victoria Prever

ZCHUG

Israel's top condiment, a spicy sauce put on EVERYTHING, came with the wave of Yemenite immigrants. It's a bit like salsa, or chutney, redolent of Middle Eastern spices, and utterly delicious with eggs, chicken, couscous, soup, fish, and soft, freshly baked pitta. It keeps up to 2 weeks in the refrigerator. It may be frozen but loses much of its freshness and oomph —best eaten within a few days of preparing.

In the summer when tomatoes are fresh and sweet-ripe, use those. The rest of the year, tinned tomatoes are fine. I like eating zchug in spring because it is as light as it is vivacious, priming my palate for the lighter foods of spring and summer. Also because fresh coriander, parsley, and mint are just beginning to go wild in my garden! I add fresh mint to my version, though it's not traditional.

PARVE/ MAKES APPROXIMATELY 500ML /2 CUPS

5-8 cloves garlic, chopped
2-3 medium hot chillies, such as jalapeno, or several spoonfuls of
hot chilli condiment of choice from a bottle, tin, or jar: harissa,
Chinese chilli garlic paste, tabasco, to taste (they all have a different
heat level, some mild, others nearly lethal!)
400g/14oz tin chopped tomatoes and their juices
1 small bunch coriander, chopped • ½ bunch parsley, chopped
Handful fresh mint, chopped • 2 teaspoons ground cumin, or to taste
½ teaspoon turmeric, or to taste • Seeds from 5-6 cardamom pods
½ teaspoon fragrant curry powder • ¼ teaspoon ground ginger, or to taste
2 tablespoons extra virgin olive oil • Juice of ½ lemon
Salt to taste

Either in a bowl or food processor, combine all of the ingredients.

Whizz the ingredients together for a smooth sauce, or for a chunkier version, hand chop all the ingredients then simply stir together.

Taste for seasoning, then place in a bowl, cover and chill in the refrigerator until ready to serve.

Marlena Spieler

CHIRSHI – SPICY TRIPOLITAN PUMPKIN PASTE

Chirshi is a well-seasoned pumpkin paste, traditionally served as an appetizer accompanied by very thick slices of simple bread or challah. The secret of this dish is to maintain the incandescent orange of the pumpkin by avoiding overcooking, or over-seasoning it – but seasoning should nonetheless be applied generously. Therefore, although normally quantities in Israeli cuisine are of a rather flexible nature (for Israelis are notoriously disobedient), it is important to follow the quantities and preparation instructions mentioned in this recipe, strictly.

PARVE /SERVES 10

350g/3 cups fresh pumpkin, cubed • 1 sweet potato, peeled and chopped
3 carrots, peeled and chopped • 4 garlic cloves
1 tablespoon hot paprika • 2 tablespoons ground caraway seeds
Salt • Juice of 1 lemon • 6 tablespoons olive oil

Cook pumpkin, sweet potato and carrots in boiling water until carrots are soft. Drain through a colander and leave to stand in order to get rid of any excess water.

Roughly mash the vegetables using a fork (not a food processor!) together with the rest of the ingredients. Leave a few chunks.

Taste and adjust seasoning.

Serve hot or cold with plenty of fresh bread.

Gil Hovav

MAIN DISHES

ROASTED PAPRIKA CHICKEN, WHITE RICE WITH NUT AND RAISIN TOPPING

My home cooking is of Iraqi origin where nuts and raisins feature in many of our recipes for festivals and happy occasions. This recipe evokes memories of the warm atmosphere created in our house whenever there was a family celebration; red chicken and rice with lots of fried onion, dried fruit and nuts. It is delicious, colourful and looks fantastic. Serve with green vegetables and a salad.

MEATY /SERVES 4

For the chicken
4 chicken leg quarters, thigh and leg • 4-6 tablespoons olive oil, not extra virgin
Paprika, hot, sweet or a blend – whatever suits your palate
2-3 teaspoons salt • 8 cloves garlic, peeled and crushed • 1-2 onions, chopped

For the rice
390g/2 cups of basmati rice, washed in cold water and drained
3 tablespoons olive oil, not extra virgin • Salt • Water

For the rice topping
1 large onion (or 2 small) • 2-3 tablespoons olive oil, not extra virgin
2 tablespoons raisins • 2 tablespoons flaked almonds
2 tablespoons pine nuts or any other nuts of your choice • Salt, pepper

Season the chicken with olive oil, paprika, garlic, onion and salt. Massage it with your hands until the chicken is well coated.Place the chicken pieces in a tray. Put it in a hot oven at 200°C/400°F/ gas 6 for about 45 minutes, or until golden brown and cooked through.

Put the rice into a saucepan. Add cold tap water. The water should cover the rice by 2cm/1 inch. Add salt (about 1 tablespoon) and olive oil. Stir, bring to a boil, and stir again.

When most of the water has evaporated and a few 'dimples' have appeared, turn the heat down, cover and let cook for around 10-15 minutes or until the rice is soft to the bite and fluffy.

Shallow sauté the onion in the olive oil, season with salt and black pepper until golden and add the raisins. Cook for another 2-3 minutes for the raisins to absorb the flavours.

In a separate frying pan, toss the almonds and pine nuts until golden.

Add the nuts to the onions and raisins, and mix together.

Simi Goldberg

POJO CON BIZELAS
CHICKEN WITH PEAS

When fresh peas are sweet, they are a seasonal delight that make this dish both beautiful to look at and delicious to eat. However, even in spring, not all fresh peas are tender and sweet, so if the sample pea you taste at the market is starchy, it is perfectly all right to use frozen peas. They are usually consistently sweet and tender. The celery is not essential but it does contribute moisture and a certain leafy quality to the dish. This is very much like an old Portuguese recipe called *frango com ervilhas*. In the older recipe, sautéed onions are added and a bit of dry port or Madeira. The dill or mint is a Turkish touch. I think some sautéed spring onions/scallions would not be remiss in this dish, and I would add them when I add the celery and fresh peas.

MEATY /SERVES 6-8

1 large frying chicken or 2 young fryers, each about 1 kg/2lb
cut into serving pieces
Flour • Salt and freshly ground black pepper • Oil
250ml/1 cup water or chicken broth as needed
75g/½ cup chopped spring onion/scallions, optional
8 stalks celery, cut in 5cm /2-inch pieces
900g/2lb shelled English peas, or 600g/20oz frozen baby peas, thawed
2 teaspoons sugar, optional • 4–6 tablespoons chopped fresh dill or mint

Combine flour, salt and pepper on a plate. Film a heavy sauté pan with oil and dip the chicken pieces in the seasoned flour, then shake off the excess flour. Fry chicken over medium high heat until golden on all sides. If necessary, do this in batches so you don't crowd the chicken in the pan.

Transfer the chicken to one large stew pot, add water or broth, bring to a boil and reduce heat. Simmer covered for 20 minutes.

Add the spring onions, if using, the celery, fresh peas and herbs and simmer until chicken is tender – approximately 15 to 20 minutes longer. If using thawed frozen peas, add them during the last 5 minutes. Adjust seasoning, adding sugar if you think the peas warrant the additional sweetness.

Place the chicken on a serving platter and spoon the sauce, peas and celery over the top. Serve with rice or noodles.

Joyce Goldstein

SHAWARMA SALAD

This dish, together with its rice component, is an entire delicious meal in itself. The inspiration for the recipe came from the Comme il Faut restaurant in the Tel Aviv Port. I immediately fell in love with its name and when I came home I prepared my own very simple version of it – the one you see here. I promise this recipe will become part of your personal repertoire.

MEATY /SERVES 4

4 chicken breasts • 200g/1 cup long grain white rice • Juice of 2 lemons
1 large red onion, sliced into very thin rings
½ bunch parsley, discarding stalks
1 green chilli pepper, seeds removed and thinly sliced

Marinade
1 teaspoon turmeric • 1 teaspoon sweet or hot paprika (season to taste)
1 teaspoon cumin • 4 tablespoons olive oil
½ teaspoon salt • Black pepper

Place all marinade ingredients in a large bowl together with the chicken breasts and marinate for at least 30 minutes in the refrigerator. Meanwhile, cook the rice.

Soak the red onion rings in the juice of the two lemons to soften the rings and bring out the oniony bite. Fry the chicken breasts in a skillet (frying pan) until they are dark brown on both sides. Slice into short, thin strips.

Add the parsley leaves, sliced chilli pepper and rice to the onion rings and lemon juice. Add salt and mix well. Scatter the shawarma pieces on top and mix well so that the shawarma takes on the lemony flavour.

Serve immediately or cold.

Michal Ansky

POLLO EZECHIELE – CHICKEN WITH TOMATOES, OLIVES, HERBS AND RED WINE

Many dishes in Italian Jewish cooking have a first name associated with it and this dish has a Biblical one: the prophet Ezekiel! I first came across this dish in *La cucina nella tradizione ebraica*, and this is my adaptation of it. It is easy to make and always a success, with great depth of flavours and a scent of Mediterranean cooking.

MEATY /SERVES 4-6

4-6 serving pieces of chicken, skin on • 4-5 tablespoons extra virgin olive oil
2 cloves garlic, crushed • Handful pitted black olives
Small bunch fresh sage • Small bunch fresh rosemary
Small bunch fresh basil • 1 bay leaf
400g/14oz tin plum tomatoes in tomato juice • 125ml/½ cup red wine
Salt and freshly ground black pepper to taste

Clean and rinse the chicken thoroughly, pat it dry and cut it, if necessary, into serving size pieces. Warm the oil in a large non-stick frying pan. Add the chicken and let it sauté, covered, until golden on all sides at medium-high heat for a few minutes.

Once the chicken has turned golden, add the garlic, olives, pre-washed herbs (leave a few aside for decoration), tomatoes with their juice, and a little salt and pepper. Stir, reduce the flame to low and cover. Leave the chicken to cook until tender for approximately 30 minutes. Check if the chicken is cooked by piercing its meat. If there is pink juice coming out it is not yet cooked. Cook for another 5-10 minutes and then check again until the juice is clear.

Once the chicken is cooked, uncover the pan and add the red wine. Raise the heat, stir and leave the wine to evaporate for a couple of minutes. The sauce should now be thick and full of flavour.

Spoon out any extra oil, or fat, as a result of the cooking and transfer to a warmed platter. You can also remove the skin if you prefer at this stage, or serve it as it is.

Sprinkle with fresh herbs for decoration, if desired. Serve hot with some rice and/or vegetables on the side. It keeps well for a couple of days in the fridge and tastes even better the next day!

Silvia Nacamulli

CHICKEN WITH GINGER AND SPRING ONION

I always feel that this dish embodies the freshness and lightness of Chinese cuisine like a spring morning. The ginger adds such a clean zest and the chicken is filling and nutritious. Please enjoy.

MEATY /SERVES 4

340g/12oz breast or leg of boned and skinned chicken
1 medium-sized onion • 2 large spring onions/scallions
Thumb-sized piece fresh ginger • 2 large cloves fresh garlic
1 tablespoon dark soy sauce • ½ teaspoon of sesame oil
1 level teaspoon white granulated sugar • 3 tablespoons pure vegetable oil
3 tablespoons Chinese rice wine • 1 level teaspoon cornflour
Salt and pepper

Dice the chicken into 1cm/½-inch cubes. Slice the onion into segments about ½cm/¼-inch wide at the outside. Cut the spring onions into 2.5cm /1-inch pieces. If the spring onions are thick, cut in half. Peel the ginger and finely slice into about 8 pieces. Finely chop the garlic until it is almost like a paste.

Marinate the chicken for 10 minutes in a bowl with the soy sauce, a few drops of sesame oil, half of the sugar, a drop of the vegetable oil, a pinch of salt and the rice wine. Mix well.

Heat a frying pan and add half the remainder of the vegetable oil. When the oil is very hot, put the chicken into the pan and stir for 1 minute, then remove the chicken and put it into a bowl. Pour the remainder of the vegetable oil into the hot pan with half of the remaining sesame oil. Put the garlic, spring onions and ginger in too and stir for 20 seconds. Add the onion and continue to stir. Add the remainder of the sugar, a few drops of dark soy sauce and a drop of rice wine. Stir for a minute, then add the chicken and cook for a further 1 minute. Keep the flame at the highest setting throughout.

Put the cornflour into a bowl with 120ml/½ cup of water with the remainder of the sesame oil and slowly pour into the pan whilst stirring. The dish is now ready for your family. Serve with chopsticks, rice and vegetables.

Philip Pell

ITALIAN CHICKEN SPIRALS

This recipe transforms a chicken breast into a delicious wrap of aubergine, basil and tomatoes, the flavours of Italy. The meat needs to be flattened and I found the best way to do this is to place the breast between two sheets of cling film or baking parchment. It can be prepared in advance and cooked at a later stage. To keep the Italian style, serve with a basil dressing.

MEATY /SERVES 4

1 aubergine, sliced thinly lengthways • 5 tablespoons olive oil
4 chicken breasts, thinly sliced and flattened
4 teaspoons sun-dried tomato paste or tomato purée
2 cloves garlic, peeled and crushed • 1 egg, for coating
8 tablespoons breadcrumbs • Salt and freshly ground black pepper

Basil Dressing
75g/2½oz pine nuts • Large bunch fresh basil
2 cloves garlic, peeled and roughly chopped
100ml/a little bit less than ½ cup olive oil
Salt and freshly ground black pepper
Garnish: Sprigs of basil, 4 cherry tomatoes sliced

Preheat the grill to its highest setting.

Place the aubergine slices on a baking tray. Drizzle over 3 tablespoons olive oil and grill for 5 minutes on each side or until golden.

Place the chicken breasts on a board. If too thick, flatten them by placing between 2 sheets of non-stick baking parchment paper and gently bashing with a rolling pin.

Spread each chicken breast with sun-dried tomato paste, then an aubergine slice and top with a few basil leaves and a sprinkling of salt and freshly ground black pepper and crushed garlic.

Denise Phillips

Roll up firmly and secure with a cocktail stick. Brush with a little beaten egg and sprinkle with breadcrumbs.

Heat the remaining 2 tablespoons of olive oil. Sauté the chicken breasts for about 3 minutes on each side or until golden.

Place the spirals on a baking tray.

Preheat the oven to 200°C/400°F/gas 6.

Cook for 25-30 minutes, or until thoroughly cooked.

DRESSING

Roast the pine nuts in a dry frying pan for 2-3 minutes. They will cook fast so keep an eye on them.

Remove immediately and transfer to another dish.

Place the pine nuts, basil and garlic in the food processor. Blitz together so that it forms a paste.

Gradually add the olive oil and season to taste.

NOTE

To serve the stylish way: place the chicken spirals on a warmed plate, drizzle over some basil dressing and garnish with sprigs of basil.

POT-COOKED SPRING CHICKEN WITH YOUNG VEGETABLES

Serve with baked or boiled potatoes. Mère Brazier served her pot-cooked chicken with Dijon mustard and cornichons on the table – I recommend it.

MEATY /SERVES 4

1 spring chicken, weighing about 1.5kg/3½lb • 1 sprig thyme • 1 bay leaf
1 tablespoon oil • 2 small shallots, peeled and left whole
16 young carrots, stalks removed, and other new season vegetables:
green beans, peas, fennel, young new potatoes, small turnips
Sea salt and black pepper • 500ml/2 cups chicken stock or water
Parsley to serve (optional)

Preheat the oven to 200°C/400°F/gas 6.

Pull out any fat on the opening of the chicken cavity and discard.

Put the herbs inside the cavity, truss the chicken tightly with string and rub with oil.

Put it in a casserole and tuck the shallots and carrots around it. Season with salt and pepper and pour the stock around it.

Cover with a lid and cook in the oven for 45 minutes.

Remove the lid and cook for a further 20 minutes. Taste the cooking juices and season with a little more salt if necessary.

STEW OF LAMB AND HONEY

The beginning of spring is strongly associated with lambs in pasture. For me it's also a reminder of Passover, Chag he-Aviv. As a young girl growing up before the Second World War, I can still evoke the memory of my mother preparing a beautiful lamb stew for the first Seder night and the delicious smell which filled our home. As a side dish, my mother would serve tutti-frutti which I have replaced with a gorgeous apple and apricot compote.

MEATY /SERVES 4

500g/1lb lamb shoulder • 1 onion • 100g/3½oz whole, peeled almonds
2 tablespoons oil • 1 teaspoon ground cinnamon
2 tablespoons honey • 1 tablespoon sesame seeds
Salt and black pepper

Dice the lamb. Peel and finely chop the onion. Roughly chop the almonds.

Heat the oil in a large frying pan until very hot. Add the lamb and fry over a high heat, stirring now and then, until all the pieces of lamb are well browned. Add the ground cinnamon and season well with salt and pepper. Cover the lamb pieces with enough water so that the water level is 2.5cm/1 inch over the lamb. Cover the pan and simmer for at least 45 minutes.

Add the honey, half of the chopped almonds and half of the sesame seeds. Mix all ingredients together. Simmer for 15 more minutes.

For the garnish, heat a small, dry pan over medium heat. Roast the other half of the leftover sesame seeds and chopped almonds for three to four minutes. Shake the pan every 20 seconds or stir with a wooden spoon to ensure they roast evenly. Before serving, sprinkle the roasted almonds and sesame seeds on top of the lamb stew.

NOTE

Delicious served with boiled potatoes, rice or couscous and a side dish of apple and apricot compote (see page 127).

Nanny ten Brink-de Lieme

PARISIENNE GNOCCHI WITH SPINACH, ONION AND POACHED EGG

I first learned of Parisienne gnocchi whilst working on a cookbook with Thomas Keller and Jeffrey Cerciello. When I read this recipe I realised that the basic dough is a choux paste rather than a traditional gnocchi. Then I thought, why not make a choux paste using schmaltz instead of butter and chicken stock instead of water to make a very savoury and flavourful dish.

MEATY /SERVES 4

240ml/1 cup chicken stock • 120g/½ cup schmaltz
1 teaspoon kosher salt • 140g/1 cup all purpose (plain) flour • 4 large eggs
4 tablespoons chopped fresh herbs • 30g/2 tablespoons schmaltz
1 Spanish onion, thinly sliced • 675g/1½lb fresh spinach, stems removed
4 large eggs • Salt and freshly ground black pepper

Combine the stock, schmaltz and salt in a medium saucepan over a high heat.

When the liquid begins to simmer, turn down the heat to medium and add the flour.

Stir continuously until all the liquid has been absorbed and a uniform paste formed. Continue to cook, stirring, for another minute or two.

Set the saucepan aside to cool for five minutes.

Crack an egg into the pan and quickly stir to combine. It will be slick at first but the paste will soon embrace the egg. Repeat with the remaining eggs.

Stir in the herbs.

Fill a large saucepan with water and bring to the boil.

Michael Ruhlman

Invert a large zipper-top plastic bag over your hand and use it to gather up all the choux paste, then re-invert the bag with the paste inside. Snip 1.25cm/½-inch off one corner of the bag and pipe the dough into the simmering stock, cutting the gnocchi off at 4cm/1½-inch lengths.

The gnocchi are ready as soon as they float to the surface. Drain them well and toss them into a little oil or schmaltz to prevent them from sticking together. You can chill or freeze the gnocchi at this stage.

Bring a large pot of water to a simmer for the poached eggs.

Melt the schmaltz in a large frying pan over medium heat and fry the onion until completely cooked and slightly coloured.

Add the gnocchi to the pan along with more schmaltz to help them brown. Fry for 4 or 5 minutes until the gnocchi are golden brown.

Add the spinach to the pan and cook until it has wilted. Season well.

Poach the eggs in the pot of simmering water.

Give it all a pinch of salt and several grinds of pepper.

Divide the gnocchi and spinach among 4 warm plates, and top each with a poached egg. Give the eggs one last pinch of salt and a grind of pepper and serve.

LAMB WITH GREEN GARLIC

Spring is the season for green garlic, fragrant shoots with tiny young bulbs. Before individual cloves are formed, the green garlic resembles large scallions or baby leeks. Combined with spring green onions they make for a delicate and aromatic stew. If you cannot find green garlic at your market, use peeled cloves from 2 small heads of garlic instead. With the slow cooking, the cloves will become mild and creamy. Serve with rice or roast potatoes.

MEATY /SERVES 6-8

Plain flour • Salt and freshly ground black pepper • Olive oil
1½-2 kg/3-4lb lamb shoulder cut into 3.5cm /1½-inch pieces
2 tablespoons tomato paste • 2 tablespoons vinegar
240ml/1 cup water or meat broth
225g/8oz green garlic or 2 heads garlic, peeled, cloves separated
1kg/2lb spring onions/scallions, about 5 or 6 bunches • 5 tablespoons oil

On a plate, combine flour with salt and pepper. Cover the base of a large heavy sauté pan with olive oil over a high heat. Dip the lamb in seasoned flour and fry in batches in oil until browned on all sides.

Transfer the lamb to a heavy stew pot, add the tomato paste, vinegar, broth or water, salt and pepper and bring to a boil. Reduce heat to a simmer and cover the pan. Cook slowly over low heat for 50 to 60 minutes.

Do not peel the green garlic but snip off the root end and slice into 5cm/2-inch lengths, using all of the green. Or peel the cloves of garlic from 2 small heads. Trim the roots off the spring onions and also cut them into 5cm/2-inch lengths. Blanch the spring onions in boiling salted water for 2 minutes, then drain.

Sauté the garlic and spring onions in a few tablespoons of olive oil over moderate heat for approximately 5 minutes, just to get a bit of colour on them, seasoning them with salt and pepper.

After about 1 hour, when the lamb is almost cooked, add the garlic and green onions to the pot. Cover and continue to cook until lamb is tender, another 20 or 30 minutes. Adjust seasoning. Sprinkle with chopped mint, dill or parsley and serve at once.
(Picture on page 67)

Joyce Goldstein

GREEK LAMB STEW WITH ROMAINE LETTUCE AND DILL

My aunt Rosa Miller who grew up in Thessaloniki, Greece, cooked delicious food in the Sephardic inspired Greek tradition and this dish is an apotheosis of spring flavours: lamb, lemon, lettuce and dill. The lettuce makes it utterly unlike any lamb stew I know of.

MEATY /SERVES 6

800g/1¾lb lean lamb (from the leg) • Salt and freshly ground pepper
1 tablespoon extra-virgin olive oil • 4 large heads romaine lettuce, separated
into leaves, washed and spun dry • 1 bunch of fresh dill, finely chopped
1 bunch of spring onions/scallions, trimmed and finely chopped
6 tablespoons fresh lemon juice (2 lemons) • 1 teaspoon sugar

Trim fat and sinews from lamb and cut into 3.5cm/1½-inch cubes. Season well with salt and pepper.

Heat the oil in a large non-stick sauté pan and thoroughly brown the lamb on all sides over high heat. Pour off and discard fat from pan.

Return lamb to the pan and add 500ml/2 cups of water. Bring lamb to boil, reduce the heat and cover the pan. Gently simmer the lamb for about an hour until tender. Add water to keep lamb moist.

Remove lamb, and keep cooking liquid in pan.

Cut lettuce leaves into 5cm/2-inch squares. Add the diced lettuce, dill, scallions and lemon juice to the pan with the cooking liquid. Simmer until the lettuce is tender (approximately 5 minutes).

Return the lamb to the pan and simmer until thoroughly heated. Add the sugar, salt and pepper to taste.

Steven Raichlen

SUMAC RACK OF LAMB WITH FATTOUSH SALAD

When I think of spring food, lamb always comes to mind, and for this recipe I've added some Middle Eastern flavours. Fattoush is one of my favourite salads to order in the Lebanese restaurants in London's Edgware Road. I love the light, lemony freshness of the salad, and I think it goes perfectly alongside the garlic and sumac lamb – they remind me of the summer to come. I had to put pomegranate molasses into the dressing as I can't have enough of its sour, sweet and fruity flavour. When I make this dish, I usually cut up a few extra pittas – the crisps are delicious dipped in hummus, and are great to serve to your guests before you sit down to a meal.

MEATY /SERVES 4

For the lamb
4 racks of lamb, French trimmed, and fat removed
(approx. 200g/7oz per person)
1 tablespoon ground sumac • 2 garlic cloves, crushed
Olive oil • Sea salt • Black pepper

For the salad
4 wholemeal pitta breads • 1 cos or iceberg lettuce, sliced
Handful rocket leaves • 1 bunch vine tomatoes, quartered
1 bunch radishes, thinly sliced
2 Lebanese cucumbers or 1 regular, halved lengthways and sliced
½ small red onion, very finely sliced • 1 spring onion/scallion, finely sliced
Small handful flat leaf parsley, roughly chopped
Small handful fresh mint leaves, roughly chopped

For the dressing
1 tablespoon ground sumac • 2 tablespoons pomegranate molasses
Zest and juice of 2 lemons • 4 tablespoons extra virgin olive oil
1 garlic clove, crushed • Sea salt • Black pepper

Rachel Davies

Preheat the oven to 180°C/350°F/gas 4.

With scissors, cut the pitta bread into triangle-shaped pieces, and split each triangle into 2 thinner pieces along its natural break. Place on a baking tray lined with baking paper, drizzle with olive oil, sea salt and pepper, and bake for about 10 minutes, or until crisp and golden.

Combine the dressing ingredients in a bowl, and whisk together. Season with salt and pepper, and leave for the flavours to develop.

For the lamb topping, make a paste with the sumac, crushed garlic and a splash of olive oil.

Put an oven-proof frying pan over a high heat. Add a tablespoon of oil to the pan, and when it is really hot, add the lamb, meat side down. Leave until lightly golden, and then seal the meat for about 2 minutes on each side, leaving it to brown a little. If you have a pair of tongs, these will help to turn the meat.

Remove from the heat, and using a spoon, smear the sumac paste over the lamb.

Roast the lamb in the oven-proof pan for 10 minutes for rare, 15 minutes for medium, or 20 minutes for well done. When the meat is ready, let it rest covered in foil for about 10 minutes.

Mix together the salad ingredients and the herbs in a large bowl.

Just before serving, whisk and pour most of the dressing over the salad and toss well.

Serve the lamb and salad with the pitta crisps sprinkled on top, and a little extra dressing to drizzle.

NOTE

For a more substantial meal you could serve bulgur wheat or couscous sprinkled with a little parsley and mint.

NAVARIN D'AGNEAU – FRENCH LAMB STEW

An Irish stew is perhaps the best-known lamb ragoût in the world, but a *navarin d'agneau* is the best-tasting one. Over the years, I've taught this recipe in many cities throughout the country, and often had students tell me that at least one member of their family wouldn't eat lamb. They checked the recipe further and found the turnips. Now matters were much worse, for no one in their family ate turnips! Can the turnips be left out? Not if the stew is to be a *navarin*. Luckily, my students went home, followed the recipe, and re-created what they had tasted in class. The reports that came back were not only that the *navarin* was a success, but that 'they even wanted more turnips'. If you are among those who do not like lamb or turnips, be encouraged that you are in for a tasty surprise. As with any stew, this not only can be made ahead of time, but it improves with age.

As in *boeuf bourguignon*, this is one place where using a leaner cut of meat will detract from the recipe. The lamb shoulder's fat content will produce moist and tender meat. Your butcher may suggest boned leg of lamb instead, but you should insist on the shoulder.

MEATY /SERVES 6

4 tablespoons vegetable oil
1 kg/2½lb boned shoulder of lamb (see Note), trimmed and cut into
3.5cm/1½-inch cubes • 30g/¼ cup all-purpose (plain) flour
750ml/3 cups beef stock, homemade or canned
250ml/1 cup dry white wine • 1 tablespoon tomato paste
3 cloves garlic, finely chopped • Bouquet garni • ¼ teaspoon salt
¹/₈ teaspoon freshly ground pepper
4 large carrots, cut into 2.5cm/1-inch pieces
18 pearl onions, peeled, root end trimmed but left intact
to hold the onions together
3 small to medium white turnips, peeled and quartered
18 small Yukon Gold potatoes, peeled • Chopped parsley, for garnish

In a large flameproof casserole, heat 3 tablespoons of the oil over high heat until it begins to smoke. Add the cubes of lamb and brown well on all sides, turning the pieces only after they have browned. If your casserole is not large enough to hold the lamb in one layer, this can be

Richard Grausman

done in two batches.

Sprinkle the flour over the meat and brown over medium heat, 3 to 5 minutes.

Add the stock, wine, tomato paste, garlic, and bouquet garni. Stir with a wooden spoon. Season with the salt and pepper. Bring to a boil, then reduce the heat to medium-low, cover, and simmer.

Meanwhile, in a 25-30cm /10-12-inch frying pan (skillet), heat the remaining 1 tablespoon of oil over high heat. Add the carrots and brown, shaking the skillet frequently. Remove the carrots and set aside. Next, brown the pearl onions and turnips in the same skillet.

After the lamb has been simmering for 30 minutes, add the browned carrots. After another 15 minutes, add the onions and turnips. Check both meat and vegetables for tenderness from time to time, and if one of the vegetables is fully cooked before the rest, remove it to prevent overcooking. Whilst everything is gently cooking, skim off all the fat and impurities that come to the surface. Total cooking time will be about 1½ hours. (The stew can be made several days ahead to this point. Remove the bouquet garni. Let cool to room temperature, cover, and refrigerate or freeze. Bring slowly back to a simmer whilst you cook the potatoes; see next step.)

Boil or steam the potatoes until they are tender, about 20 minutes. (If boiled, drain them.) Add them to the casserole when all ingredients are tender, and cook 5 minutes longer.

Skim any fat remaining on the sauce, adjust the seasoning if necessary, and remove the bouquet garni. Transfer the stew to a hot serving dish and sprinkle with chopped parsley just before serving.

NOTE

Turning vegetables: In many classic dishes, vegetables are 'turned' (pared into uniform football or olive shapes) to add to the attractiveness of a dish. In France, the vegetables in a *navarin d'agneau* or other ragoûts would be turned, but it's not worth doing unless you think your guests will appreciate it. To turn large root vegetables (potatoes, turnips, carrots), first cut them into chunks, then trim them to an olive shape with a paring knife. This takes practice.

VARIATION
Navarin Printanier – French Lamb Stew with Spring Vegetables

This version of a *navarin* takes its name from the springtime (*printanier*) vegetables that are added to it. In step 6, along with the cooked potatoes, add about 225g/8oz cooked peas and 100g/4oz cooked green beans. Serving Suggestion: When serving *navarin d'agneau*, I often start with a green salad and finish with a pastry like Choux Soufflés au Chocolat. Wine–Red Bordeaux.

SPRING LAMB CASSEROLE

When I grew up in wartime, there were no exotic vegetables like aubergines or sugar snap peas. Meat was rationed so when it eventually became available again, when I was in my teens, it was a huge treat to taste the first spring lamb. The editor of one of my early cookbooks, *The Essential Jewish Cookbook,* wanted hearty winter stews but I love the lighter flavours of fresh vegetables with a hint of garlic and rosemary. The peas and beans used here are frozen. Later in the year, you can buy them in their pods for extra flavour.

MEATY /SERVES 4

4 tablespoons olive oil • 2 onions, peeled and quartered
2 cloves garlic, crushed • 4 large or 12 baby carrots, peeled
1½ kg/3 lb lamb shoulder on the bone • ½ beef stock cube
450g/1lb frozen peas or same weight fresh podded ones
450g/1lb frozen broad beans • Salt and black pepper
1kg/2lb small new potatoes • Few sprigs fresh rosemary

Heat half the olive oil in a large pan and when it is hot, sauté the onions until they begin to brown.

Cut up the carrots if they are large and add them to the pan. Cook for another few minutes then move the vegetables to a casserole.

Add the rest of the olive oil, put in the lamb and brown it on all sides. Season with the crushed garlic, salt and pepper.

Judy Jackson

Crumble over the beef stock cube and pour over enough boiling water to come halfway up the meat. Bubble for a few minutes, then transfer the meat with the liquid to the casserole.

Cover and cook in a moderate oven 180°C/350°F/gas 4 for about 1 hour. Test to see that there is enough liquid to make gravy and add a little more if needed. Continue cooking for a further 30 minutes or until the meat is tender.

Cook the frozen peas and beans separately for about five minutes in boiling salted water. Remove the skins from the broad beans. (If you are using fresh vegetables, take them out of their pods and cook as above.)

Serve the lamb with the peas, beans and some boiled new potatoes (or you could roast them in a little oil in a separate pan for about an hour whilst the lamb is cooking).

NOTE

Serving idea: arrange the meat and the vegetables on a platter and garnish with fresh rosemary. To improve the dish, you can remove the fat which forms on the gravy. At the end of the cooking, pour the gravy into a bowl, leave to cool and freeze for about an hour. Remove the layer of fat which will have formed at the top and then pour the gravy back into the casserole. Bring the meat, carrots and onions back to the boil before serving.

ROASTED BEET SALAD WITH MINT

I love beets – they're sweet, succulent, colourful, and healthy. The beets we eat today are thought to have evolved from a prehistoric North African root vegetable. Originally people only ate the greens at the top of the beet. In Ancient Rome, people began to cultivate the root itself for consumption. Beetroot became more popular as a food source during the 16th century. The flavours in this salad really pop; the freshness of the mint is a lovely counterpoint to the earthy sweetness of the roasted beets.

PARVE /SERVES 8

1kg/2lb (about 6 medium) roasted red beets, skins removed
3 tablespoons balsamic vinegar • 2 tablespoons olive oil
2 teaspoons sugar • ¼ teaspoon cumin
¼ teaspoon salt (or more to taste) • 5g/¼ cup fresh chopped mint

Chop roasted beets into bite-sized pieces and place them in a salad bowl.

Whisk together the vinegar, oil, sugar, cumin and salt.

Pour dressing over the beets, then add 3 tablespoons chopped mint. Toss salad gently until beets are coated in the dressing and mint.

Sprinkle the last tablespoon of mint over the top of the salad. Serve.

NOTE

This salad can be made ahead, but the mint must be added just before serving, otherwise the beet juices will turn the mint red. If you are preparing this salad gluten free, make sure you use a certified gluten-free balsamic vinegar. This salad is a versatile side dish that will compliment a variety of dishes. The sweet, robust flavour pairs particularly well with goat's cheese and cheese sauces, smoked fish, nuts and lentils.

Tori Avey

BEEF IN BLACK BEAN SAUCE WITH GREEN PEPPER

Stir-fried Chinese food is cooked over a really hot flame in a wok that spreads the heat evenly. Cooking on a conventional stove will not produce the intensity of heat therefore the cooking will be slower and the results different from the dish you would taste at Kaifeng restaurant.

MEATY /SERVES 4

350g/12oz of rib eye beef • 1 medium onion • 1 large green pepper
3 cloves garlic • 2 spring onions/scallions • 2 tablespoons light soy sauce
1 small teaspoon sugar • ½ teaspoon black pepper
3 tablespoons pure vegetable oil • 1 teaspoon sesame oil
½ teaspoon salt • 2 tablespoons black beans
2 small red chillies (optional) • 1 teaspoon cornflour

Slice the beef into thin strips and dice the onion and green pepper into very small pieces. Crush the garlic and cut the spring onions/scallions into very small strips.

First marinate the beef for 15 minutes, using half of the soy sauce, half of the sugar, half of the black pepper, a third of the vegetable oil and half of the sesame oil.

Heat your wok and pour in a third of the vegetable oil and heat until the oil is sizzling hot. Throw in half the garlic, stir for a few seconds, add the marinated beef and stir until the beef loses its red colour, but be careful not to overcook.

Take the beef out of the wok and put in a bowl. Add the remainder of the vegetable oil to the wok, put in the rest of the garlic, black beans, diced onion and green peppers. Stir fry them for 2 minutes. If you like this dish a little spicy, put in the chillies (whole for not too spicy, sliced for spicy).

Now add the remaining soy sauce, salt and sugar and continue to stir. Add the beef and stir for a few seconds. Take 125ml/½ cup of water and put the cornflour and the rest of the sesame oil in the water and stir. Then spread this evenly in the wok and continue to stir until the sauce thickens and then the dish is ready to serve with rice and vegetables.

Philip Pell

MEATBALLS WITH BROAD BEANS & LEMON

Fresh, sharp and very, very, tasty, these meatballs are our idea of the perfect spring supper dish. Serve them with orzo or Basmati rice and there isn't need for much else. Whole blanched almonds would be a good addition, for the texture. Add them to the pan along with the unshelled broad beans.

MEATY /SERVES 6

For the meatballs

300g/10oz minced beef • 150g/5oz minced lamb
1 medium onion, finely chopped • 120g/4oz breadcrumbs
2 tablespoons flat leaf parsley chopped, plus ½ tablespoon for garnish
2 tablespoons mint chopped, plus ½ tablespoon for garnish
2 tablespoons dill chopped, plus ½ tablespoon for garnish
2 tablespoons coriander chopped, plus ½ tablespoon for garnish
2 large garlic cloves, crushed • 1 tablespoon baharat spice mix
1 tablespoon ground cumin • 2 teaspoons capers, chopped
1 egg, beaten • 4½ tablespoons olive oil, for frying

For the broad beans & lemon

350g/12oz broad beans, fresh or frozen • 4 whole thyme sprigs
6 garlic cloves, sliced
8 spring onions, cut at an angle into 2cm/1 inch segments
2½ tablespoons lemon juice • 500ml/2 cups chicken stock

Yotam Ottolenghi and Sami Tamimi

Place all of the meatball ingredients (except the 4½ tablespoons olive oil) in a large mixing bowl. Add ¾ teaspoon of salt and plenty of black pepper and mix well with your hands. Form into balls about the same size as ping-pong balls.

Heat 1 tablespoon of the olive oil in an extra-large frying pan for which you have a lid. Sear half the meatballs over a medium heat, turning them until they are brown all over, about 5 minutes. Remove, add another ½ tablespoon of olive oil to the pan and cook the other batch of meatballs. Remove from the pan and wipe it clean.

While the meatballs are cooking, throw the broad beans into a pot with plenty of salted boiling water and blanch for 2 minutes. Drain and refresh under cold water. Remove the skins from half the broad beans and discard the shells.

Heat the remaining olive oil in the same pan in which you seared the meatballs. Add the thyme, garlic and spring onions and sauté over medium heat for 3 minutes. Add the unshelled broad beans, 1½ tablespoons of lemon juice, 80ml/¼ cup of the stock, ¼ teaspoon of salt and plenty of black pepper. The beans should be almost covered with liquid. Cover the pan and cook over a low heat for 10 minutes.

Return the meatballs to the pan with the broad beans. Add the remaining stock, cover the pan and simmer gently for 25 minutes. Taste the sauce and adjust the seasoning. If it is very runny, remove the lid and reduce a little. Once the meatballs stop cooking they will soak up a lot of the juices so make sure there is still plenty of sauce at this point. You can leave the meatballs now, turn off the heat, until ready to serve.

Just before serving, reheat the meatballs and add a little water, if needed, to make enough sauce. Add the remaining herbs and tablespoon of lemon juice, the shelled broad beans and stir very gently. Serve immediately.

DUCK PASTRAMI

Many gastronomic texts from the Middle Ages and Early Modern period mention Jews curing duck and goose instead of pork. Duck not only replaces pork in salami and ham-like products, but also beef, from which this classic is normally made. It is delicious hot or cold.

MEATY /SERVES 2-3

1 duck • 2 teaspoons salt • ¼ teaspoon pink salt or instacure #1
1 teaspoon ground coriander • 1 teaspoon cracked black pepper
1 teaspoon juniper berries, crushed gently • 2 bay leaves

With a sharp boning knife remove the legs and thighs from the duck. Next remove the breasts and set aside. Keep the carcass to use for stock or some other purpose.

Rub the duck parts with salt, curing salt and the other spices. Place in a plastic bag with a waterproof zip top. Place in the refrigerator for one week, turning every day. Then remove the duck parts and brush off the spices. You will notice the meat has become dark red.

Next take a smoking kettle, essentially a 75cm/2-3 foot metal canister with a door on the bottom and a rack on the top. Start a small fire in the bottom, add wet wood shavings – preferably fruit wood. Place the duck parts on the upper rack and smoke for about 2-3 hours with the door of the smoker shut. There should be no flame at all, only a lot of smoke.

Then place the duck parts in a pan and heat through, just until the fat begins to melt. Whilst still warm, slice the duck parts (with the skin) and arrange on a salad, sandwich, or however you prefer. Good mustard is a requisite.

Ken Albala

GRILLED ISRAELI SPICED FOIE GRAS

I discovered this dish on my last trip to Tel Aviv and it's a specialty of a restaurant founded by an Azeri immigrant who built a pushcart selling grilled poultry to a restaurant frequented by politicians and the press. The dish intrigued me because foie gras, by its very nature (almost pure fat) normally bursts into flames when you grill it whereas here it doesn't. Normally associated with haute French cuisine, in this unusual recipe the spicing comes from Yemen and it's grilled over charcoal utterly without pretence.

MEATY /SERVES 6

1 tablespoon coarse salt (kosher or sea) • 1 tablespoon sweet paprika
1 teaspoon ground turmeric • 1 teaspoon ground cumin
1 teaspoon freshly ground black pepper
1 teaspoon freshly ground white pepper • ½ teaspoon cayenne pepper
675g/1½lb foie gras • Pitta bread, to serve (optional)

Set up the grill for direct grilling and preheat to high.

Place the salt, paprika, turmeric, cumin and black and white peppers in a small bowl and stir to mix. Set rub aside.

Cut the foie gras into chunks. Skewer the chunks on flat metal skewers. Generously season each kebab on both sides with the rub.

Place into roasting dish to avoid fat dripping onto bottom of oven. Grill until golden brown on the outside and just cooked inside (3-5 minutes per side).

Serve at once with pitta bread.

Steven Raichlen

SLOW-BRAISED BRISKET IN CHINESE MASTER STOCK

For me, there's no time like Passover for serving brisket, when it's a mandatory star at my Seder table. Growing up, our brisket was braised in onion soup mix and canned potatoes. These days, I cook from scratch, and my tradition now incorporates the Asian influence of my adopted home of Sydney. The result? A four-hour braising of grass-fed wagyu brisket in Chinese master stock – an aromatic comfort dish that'll blow away your dinner guests. For a Sephardic-friendly Pesach, I've swapped wheat-free tamari for soy and sherry for shaoxing. If you're Ashkenazi, seek out imitation soy, or, better still, enjoy at any other time of year.

MEATY/SERVES 4-6

3 litres/12 cups water • 3 black cardamom pods, cracked open
6 pieces cassia bark, or 2 cinnamon sticks • 1 teaspoon cloves
1-2 dried chillies (optional) • 1 teaspoon fennel seeds
1 teaspoon Sichuan pepper (optional) • 4 star anise
375ml/1½ cups tamari or imitation soy sauce*
375ml/1½ cups medium-dry or pale dry sherry
1 large knob ginger (about 30g/1oz), sliced • 4 garlic cloves, peeled
3 spring onions (scallions), roughly chopped
3 pieces dried mandarin** or orange peel
200g/7oz Chinese rock sugar • 1 tablespoon vegetable or olive oil
1kg/2lb piece of brisket (preferably wagyu), halved, trimmed of excess fat

Preheat oven to 150°C/300°F/gas 2. To make the master stock, fill a stockpot with the water, then place the cardamom, cassia bark, cloves, chillies, fennel seeds, Sichuan pepper and star anise into a muslin cloth (cheesecloth), and tie with kitchen string to close. Add to the water, along with the tamari, sherry, ginger, garlic, spring onions, mandarin peel and sugar. Bring to the boil, then reduce to a low simmer and cook for 30 minutes. Remove from heat, allow to cool slightly and infuse further.

Meanwhile, heat the oil over medium-high heat in a large casserole dish (alternatively, you can use a frying pan and then transfer to a baking dish or roasting pan; separate into two dishes if needed). Brown one brisket half in the dish for several minutes on each side, do the same to the sides, then repeat with the other half.

Michael Shafran

Bring master stock back to a low boil, then add to the casserole dish (or the baking/roasting dish, if using) with both halves of brisket. Cover with a lid (or tightly with foil) and place in the oven. Braise for 2 hours, then turn both pieces over and swap places. Cook for 2 hours further.

Remove dish from the oven, then remove brisket and set aside to rest. When ready, slice into thick (about 2cm /1 inch) lengthways slices against the grain. Serve with a little of the master stock for gravy. (Strain the remaining gravy and store in the freezer to use for another day.)

NOTE

*Kosher for Passover imitation soy is made by brands such as Glicks and Haddar, and sourced from sites like isralisuper.com. Spain's Tio Pepe is among those making kosher for Passover sherry.
** I can't always find dried mandarin, so when they're in season, I'll just peel a few fresh mandarin and leave the rind pieces to completely dry next to a sunny window. Then I just put them in a glass jar to use any time a recipe calls for them.

TIP

A master stock is meant to be reused, and can last for years, if not decades – some in China are rumoured to be more than 100 years old. So once you make this dish, feel free to finely strain the liquid, discarding any solids, and place it in the freezer. The next time you want to use it, replenish it with water, a new batch of stock ingredients (relative to the amount of liquid you add) and bring it to the boil for a few minutes to kill any potential bacteria. The stock then gets more and more complex each time you use it. The only other rule is to use it for the same kind of meat, so if you start using it for beef, only reuse it for beef.

SALMON WITH NOODLES AND LEEKS

Chicken with noodles is such a popular pair but fish can be just as good. I love salmon and noodles tossed in a creamy leek and dill sauce. It is inspired by a dish I learned from Master Chef Fernand Chambrette at École de Cuisine La Varenne in Paris, where I studied and worked for nearly six years.

DAIRY /SERVES 4

3 medium leeks, split, rinsed thoroughly
1 tablespoon extra virgin olive oil or vegetable oil
Salt and freshly ground pepper to taste • 570g/1¼lb salmon fillet
80ml/⅓ cup dry white wine • 125ml/½ cup fish stock (see Note below)
80ml/⅓ cup whipping cream • 1 teaspoon dried thyme
2 tablespoons butter • 225g/8oz medium noodles
2 tablespoons chopped or snipped dill, plus a little more for sprinkling

Use white and light green parts of leeks; reserve dark green parts for making stock. Cut leeks in thin slices. Heat oil in a large skillet (frying pan). Add leeks, 1 tablespoon water, salt and pepper. Cover and cook over low heat, stirring occasionally, for about 5 minutes or until tender but not brown.

Remove skin and any bones from salmon fillet. Cut fish into small pieces.

Add wine, fish stock and cream to leeks and bring to a boil. Reduce heat to low, add fish and sprinkle lightly with salt, pepper and thyme. Cook uncovered, stirring often, for about 3 minutes or until colour of fish becomes lighter. Remove from heat.

Cut butter in pieces and put in a large heated bowl. Cook noodles uncovered in a large pot of water over high heat for about 5 minutes or until tender but firm to the bite. Drain well, transfer to bowl and toss with butter. Reheat sauce if necessary. Stir in dill. Pour over noodles and toss. Taste and adjust seasoning. Serve hot, sprinkled with a little more dill.

NOTE

To make the dish easy, I cook the salmon right in the sauce. It makes a terrific entrée for Shavuot, when dairy dishes are traditional.

For a quick fish stock, thoroughly rinse fish heads or bones and put in a saucepan with the trimmed leek tops or 1 onion, a few thyme sprigs, a bay leaf and water to cover. Bring to a boil, skim the foam, cover and cook over low heat for 20 minutes. Strain, cool and refrigerate; freeze if not using within 2 days.

Faye Levy

OODLES OF SPRING ONIONS WITH COD IN A GINGER AND SOY SAUCE

We grow all sorts of herbs and vegetables in pots on our terrace which in springtime we welcome with the same joyful enthusiasm year in year out. We truly celebrate when the first parsley, mint, rocket, lettuce, spring onions/scallions and coriander appear. A sense of happiness pervades the kitchen when these are used to make a salad or are included in other dishes. Home-grown spring onions have a wonderful soft texture and delicate taste. I heap loads on pieces of steamed fish fillets to make this simple but very tasty dish.

PARVE /SERVES 4-5

1kg/2.2lb thick cod fillets or any other firm white fish
5cm/2-inch cube fresh ginger, peeled and thinly sliced
2 big bunches of spring onions/scallions, finely shredded
200ml/1 cup sunflower oil • 120ml/½ cup soy sauce, or to taste

Cut the fish into individual portions.

Arrange on an oven-proof plate that will fit inside your steamer or on the metal grill of your wok.

Sprinkle the sliced ginger on top of each portion. Steam for about 8 minutes. When the flesh becomes opaque the fish is cooked.

Arrange the fish on a serving dish, cover with the shredded spring onions and set aside.

Heat the sunflower oil on a high heat until it begins to smoke, then immediately pour it over the spring onions and fish. The spring onions will crackle and wilt.

Drizzle the soy sauce over the top. Then tilt the dish towards you, scoop up the sauce with a spoon and baste the fish.

Serve immediately with plain boiled or steamed rice.

NOTES

The fish is also tasty the next day when eaten cold.

Linda Dangoor

MACKEREL TARTARE, HORSERADISH AND CARTA DI MUSICA

Mackerel is a plentiful and inexpensive fish with a deep earthy flavour and a firm almost meaty texture. It is high in omega 3 fatty acids and vitamin B12, both of which are rather good for you. This is an incredibly simple but very tasty dish which has been on the menu at POLPO since the very beginning and its popularity shows no sign of diminishing.

DAIRY / SERVES 4

4 mackerel fillets, skinned • ½ cucumber • Fine table salt
Caster sugar • Handful small gherkins and capers
Ground black pepper • Extra virgin olive oil • Juice of one lemon
Handful flat parsley, chopped • Creamed horseradish (to serve)
Carta di musica (to serve)

Finely dice the mackerel and set aside.

Peel and finely dice the cucumber, remove the seeds, sprinkle with salt and sugar and set aside in a colander for 1 hour to pickle.

Finely chop the gherkins and capers.

Now combine everything in a mixing bowl and season with salt, pepper, olive oil and lemon juice and add the chopped parsley. Taste and adjust seasoning if necessary.

Press equal amounts of the mixture into a 5cm/2-inch ring mould on the centre of each plate.

Serve with carta di musica (Sardinian flat bread) or other flat bread and creamed horseradish.

NOTE

This recipe requires no cooking so it is important that the fish is as fresh as possible.

Russell Norman

SHIRLEY SAVAGE'S SALMON CUTLETS

My wife, after about her second or third trip to Manchester, made this comment: 'the way your mother expresses her love for you is by cooking for you.' Despite sounding like a cliché I was struck that this was true, and that it had never occurred to me before.

There are many things of my mother's that I love: her chopped liver; her shepherd's pie; her spaghetti Bolognese, which I cooked from memory a couple of years ago, for the first time in 25 years, when we started a fleishik kitchen with Grow & Behold meat.

But somehow her salmon cutlets have a special standing. And I've learned only much more recently – from Gil Marks and others – that they have been a significant part of English Jewish cooking, and perhaps especially Mancunian Jewish cooking. Enjoy…

PARVE/SERVES 8-12

Salmon. As a kid, this was a tin of salmon, and you took it out of the can, scraped off the skin, and took out the bones. Nowadays I usually use wild salmon. Allow about 100–170g/4–6 oz per person as a main course, less if for an hors d'oeuvres. Although I've never caught a salmon, I did finally go fishing for the first time last year, and it was a good and important thing to do. Salmon are extraordinary creatures, and if you eat salmon – especially regularly – take at least some time to learn about salmon and where and how they live and die.

Onion. About half a small grated onion, per 450g/pound of salmon. Extra points if you grew them yourself, or at least know the farm they came from.

Matzo meal. Indigenous Rakusen's Matzo Meal is hard to find in NY; depending on where you are, you must make do with what there is.

Eggs. Ideally from a friend's backyard coop in Brooklyn. Cage-free organic eggs from Tesco are a reasonable second best. Don't forget to check for blood-spots.

Olive oil, salt, pepper.

Nigel Savage

Lightly cook the salmon. The easiest method is to put it in a large rectangular baking dish, a little oil on the base so it doesn't stick, and put a little salt and pepper on top. Pre-heat the oven to 200°C/400°F/gas 6 and cook for about 15 minutes. At that temperature, for that length of time, it will come out not quite fully cooked; that's as it should be.

After it's cooled down, put the salmon in a ceramic bowl and flake it. You don't want to mash it to smithereens; it should still have some sense of the texture of the salmon.

Add some grated onion and the raw egg, and mush it up, and then slowly start to add matzo meal to it – and keep mushing. You want it so that you can relatively easily form it into a ball in your hand, and for it not to fall apart in the pan. But you also don't want it to have the density of a cannonball. If too loose, add more matzo meal. If too dense, slowly add a little more onion or egg. Add salt and pepper.

When the consistency seems about right, take about a spoonful, ball it in your hand, then flatten it a little, and put it on a plate, so it'll be ready to fry. I generally do about a plate at a time – ball them, fry them, ball them, fry them…

Put about 1cm/½ inch of oil in the pan and put it on a high light. Take a little bread and put it in to see if the oil is hot enough – it should immediately sizzle on top if it is. Then fry the salmon cutlets. Turn them once. You're aiming for an incredibly yummy deep-dark-fried-but-not-burned kind of look; my mother excels at this, and after many years of practice so will you.

Take them out on a slatted spatula, and place them on what Americans call 'paper towel' but I still know as 'kitchen roll'. Allow to cool. Once done, you can also freeze them – they're extremely useful to have in the freezer for, frankly, all occasions.

TO EAT: Place on a bed of salad greens, and garnish with lemons and lemon juice.
SERVE WITH: practically anything, but especially potato salad and Hellman's mayonnaise. For extra bounce, add some wasabi powder to the mayo.
TO DRINK: you really want a viognier, and you can now get some really good kosher viognier, or viognier blends. If you drink unsupervised wine, try to find an English wine called 'Three Choirs' – this goes absolutely brilliantly with the salmon cutlets and will add a final unlikely twist to this old/new dish.

Finally: don't forget to say a bracha. For fish, that would be shehakol. And if you've never eaten my mum's salmon cutlets, you can add a shehecheyanu. Love and radical amazement never go out of style, in any time and any culture. B'tayavon…

DECONSTRUCTED SUSHI SALAD PLATTER

This wonderful fish platter is always a hit when I make it because not only does it look fabulous but it tastes just as good.

PARVE /SERVES 6

20 salmon sashimi slices • 20 smoked salmon slices
2 avocados, sliced • 5 Israeli cucumbers, julienned
1 whole lettuce, finely shredded
2 sheets nori (seaweed), cut into strips and rolled • 250ml/1 cup sushi rice
Black and white sesame seeds, for decoration

Dressing
125ml/½ cup soy sauce • 2 tablespoons rice vinegar
1 tablespoon olive oil • 2 tablespoons honey
2 teaspoons wasabi powder • Black pepper

To prepare the sushi rice, wash the rice well. Place it in a pot with 310ml/1¼ cups of cold water. Bring to a boil. Then turn the heat down and simmer on lowest heat with the lid on for about 15 minutes. Remove pot from stove and leave rice for another 10 minutes. Stir in 2 tablespoons of sushi vinegar, 1 tablespoon at a time to flavour the rice and to make it sticky. Set aside until ready to use.

The rice should be at room temperature and not cold when serving. I like serving the dressing separately to prevent the salad from becoming soggy.

Place rice in 2 sections on a platter.

In the centre, arrange the cucumbers, then the avocado slices and then the lettuce.

On the outside edges, fan the sashimi and smoked salmon and sprinkle alternately with the sesame seeds.

Serve the nori in a smaller dish and the dressing in a separate small jug.

To make the dressing whisk all ingredients together and set aside.

Sharon Glass

DILL SALMON

Some recipes are acquired through marriage, when the culinary secrets of another family become ours as well. This is credited to my sister-in-law's mother.

PARVE /SERVES 6

6 salmon fillets • 1 heaped teaspoon mustard
125ml/½ cup olive oil • 5 cloves garlic, peeled and crushed
125ml/½ cup fresh dill, chopped • 1 teaspoon onion soup mix

Preheat oven to 180°C/350°F /gas 4. Line a baking tray with parchment paper. Place fish on the baking tray.

In a small bowl, thoroughly combine mustard, olive oil, garlic, dill, and onion soup mix. Dividing mixture evenly, coat fillets.

Bake, covered, for 25 minutes.

Leah Shapira

CAPRESE LATKES

The bright colours of this dish, green, white and red, illustrate that latkes can be eaten during the spring months using seasonal produce as well as during the winter festival of Chanukah.

DAIRY /SERVES 10

3 large baking potatoes, peeled and shredded • 1 large onion, grated
2 large eggs, lightly beaten • 4 tablespoons/¼ cup matzah meal
1 teaspoon kosher salt • Oil for frying
80ml/⅓ cup balsamic vinegar • 2 tablespoons sugar
2 balls (225g/8oz each) fresh mozzarella, cut into ½cm/¼-inch thick slices
2 medium tomatoes, cut into ½cm/¼-inch thick slices • 1 bunch fresh basil
60ml/¼ cup olive oil • Freshly ground black pepper

In a large bowl stir together the potatoes, onion, matzah meal and salt.

Line a baking sheet with two layers of paper towels.

Heat enough oil to reach a depth of about ½cm/¼ inch in a large frying pan (skillet) over medium–high heat.

Form the potato mixture into 7.5cm/ 3 inch round latkes and fry in batches until crisp and browned, approx 4 to 6 minutes per side.

Transfer to the baking sheet and keep warm in a low oven.

Combine the vinegar and sugar in a small saucepan and bring to a boil over medium heat.

Lower the heat and simmer for 10 to 12 minutes until thickened.

To assemble, place one latke on each plate, top with a slice of mozzarella followed by a slice of tomato and finally a sprig of basil.

Garnish with a drizzle of the balsamic reduction and olive oil and add pepper to taste.

Jamie Geller

PUMPKIN, SPINACH AND FETA FRITTATA WITH PIPERADE

Piperade is the Southern French pepper sauce from the Basque region in South West France. The sauce is the pride and joy of a picturesque little town called Espelette, whose main claim to fame comes from its distinctive-looking long peppers, which are dried in strings and adorn the verandas and terraces of the red-shuttered houses. Having just returned from a few days away in a similarly garlanded Biarritz, it seems pertinent to include this recipe here. Piperade is often scrambled with eggs for a delicious breakfast. Frittata is the Italian version of the Spanish tortilla, the ubiquitous potato omelette, and an authentic accompaniment to the piperade.

In Australia, where I now live, frittatas are a regular feature of café menus, spiked with all manner of goodies, including olives, pumpkin, feta, spinach, potatoes, and courgettes – it's up to you.

DAIRY /SERVES 4-6

For the Frittata
8 free-range eggs • 150ml/^{2}/$_3$ cup double cream
3-4 garlic cloves, finely minced • 450g/1lb pumpkin
6 tablespoons oil • 1 teaspoon light soy sauce (optional)
Dash Tabasco • 150g/5oz baby spinach
125g/4½oz feta • 1 red onion, peeled and cut into 8 pieces

For the Piperade
2 tablespoons olive oil • 1 large yellow onion, diced
3 red peppers, grilled, skinned, de-seeded and cut into strips
3 green peppers, grilled, skinned, de-seeded and cut into strips
3-4 garlic cloves, crushed
1.35kg/3lb firm tomatoes, blanched, peeled, de-seeded and chopped
Sea salt and freshly ground black pepper
Handful of torn basil leaves

Nadine Abensur

TO MAKE THE PIPERADE

Heat the olive oil in a frying pan and sauté the onion until pale gold.

Add the strips of red and green peppers, crushed garlic, and sauté for 5 minutes on a medium heat.

Add the tomatoes and continue to sauté until they are largely broken up.

Season with sea salt and freshly ground black pepper and stir the torn basil leaves throughout.

Set aside whilst you make the frittata.

TO MAKE THE FRITTATA

Preheat the oven to 220°C/425°F/gas 7.

Crack the eggs into a bowl and whisk lightly with the double cream, salt, pepper and crushed garlic.

Leave to infuse whilst you both peel and chop the pumpkin into 2.5cm/1-inch chunks.

Baste them in an oven tray with the red onion, olive oil, soy sauce and Tabasco.

Then bake in the preheated oven for 20–25 minutes until evenly browned, caramelised and tender right through.

Transfer the pumpkin to a large, non-stick sauté pan.

On a medium heat, add the spinach to the hot pumpkin and stir through gently, until it is wilted.

Pour the egg and cream mixture on top, so that the pan is two-thirds filled.

Scatter the broken-up feta over the mixture.

Allow the egg to set, adjusting the temperature as necessary and cut through the mixture with a knife or spatula, so that the uncooked mixture can flow down and cook.

Don't stir or mix but simply move the pan gently from side to side.

Remove from the heat whilst the frittata is still slightly wobbly. Any extra setting can be done by covering with a lid, so that it sets in its own heat.

Allow to cool for 10 minutes or so and serve with the Piperade.

MAC 'N' CHEESE

For Michael and I, leaving home and being away from our mum's cooking was a real challenge during our student years. Here's one of our favourite recipes from our student cookbook. When funds are low and you're missing the luxuries of home, cook this up and get an instant cure.

DAIRY /SERVES 3

500g/1lb macaroni • Generous splash of milk
Handful of grated Cheddar and Parmesan cheese for sprinkling
2 tomatoes, thinly sliced • Salt and pepper

Cheese sauce
Large knob of butter (about 75g/2½oz) • 5 tablespoons plain flour
600ml/2½ cups milk • 100g/4oz grated Cheddar
25g/1oz grated Parmesan

To make the cheese sauce, melt the butter in a saucepan over a medium to high heat. Once it has melted, add the flour and stir well with a wooden spoon until the two ingredients are well incorporated into a roux. Cook the mixture, stirring almost constantly, for 2 minutes.

Take the saucepan off the heat, pour in a quarter of the milk and stir well until it has mixed in with the roux. Add another quarter of the milk and again stir to combine. The mixture should start to become looser now. Add a third quarter of milk and mix again before placing the pan back over the heat. Pour in the remaining milk and continue stirring with a wooden spoon until the mixture comes up to boiling point.

James and Michael Eder

Reduce the temperature to a simmer and cook, stirring, for 2-3 minutes. The sauce should become thicker.

If your white sauce hasn't thickened, then continue cooking the sauce for a little longer. Be careful and keep a close eye on the sauce because if you find that it has overcooked and burnt you will need to start afresh.

Beat in the cheese a little at a time once the sauce has thickened.

For the Mac 'n' Cheese preheat the oven to 200°C /400°C /gas 6.

Bring a large saucepan of lightly salted water to boiling point. Tip in the macaroni and cook according to the packet instructions or for about 8–10 minutes until al dente. Once cooked, drain through a colander, then tip straight into an ovenproof dish.

Pour the prepared cheese sauce over the pasta, add a good splash of milk and turn with a spoon so that the pasta is well coated in sauce.

Sprinkle over the cheese, then top with slices of tomato and season. Bake in the preheated oven for 15-20 minutes until golden and bubbling.

VARIATION

Fried mushrooms, sweet corn, truffle oil and chopped parsley are all good additions to this basic Mac 'n' Cheese recipe.

RISOTTO MARZOLINO – SPRINGTIME RISOTTO

March (Marzo) is the month when asparagus and artichokes appear at the market. Inspired by one that appears in Milka Passigli's book *Le Ricette di Casa Mia*, this festive saffron-tinged risotto uses both vegetables. Again, this dish might profit from a little grated lemon zest and chopped fresh parsley, basil or mint.

DAIRY /SERVES 6

450g/1lb asparagus • 3 large artichokes
1.5 litres/6 cups vegetable broth • ½ teaspoon saffron threads, chopped
2–3 tablespoons butter • 1 small onion, chopped
420g/2 cups Arborio rice • 250ml/1 cup double cream
45g/½ cup grated Parmesan cheese

Trim the artichokes by cutting off the stems flush to the bottoms. Remove all the leaves and cut the tender hearts in half lengthwise. Cut away the chokes, then slice the halves lengthwise in ½cm /¼ -inch -thick slices. Blanch in salted boiling water for just 2 minutes. Drain and set aside.

Pour the broth into a saucepan and bring to a simmer; adjust the heat under the broth to maintain a gentle simmer.

Ladle out 1 cup of the hot broth, place in a bowl, and add the saffron; set aside.

Melt the butter in a large sauté pan over medium heat. Add the onion and sauté until tender and translucent, about 5 to 8 minutes. Add the rice and stir until opaque, about 3 minutes. Add a ladleful of the simmering broth and stir until the broth is absorbed. Lower the heat and continue to add broth, a ladleful at a time.

For the final cup, add the saffron and its broth along with the asparagus and artichokes. Stir until the broth is absorbed and the rice kernels are al dente at the centre and creamy on the outside, 20 to 25 minutes in all. Stir in the cream and Parmesan cheese and heat through. Serve at once.

Joyce Goldstein

PIZZA EBRAICA DI ERBE – DOUBLE CRUSTED VEGETABLE PIE

Called a Jewish-style pizza, the origins of this dish are probably in the Italian south. Here the word pizza is related to the Greek pitta, a name for filo pies; a term still in use in Apulia, where many dishes reflect a Greek heritage. This recipe calls for pasta *frolla salata*, a short pastry crust which gives it a wonderful richness.

DAIRY /SERVES 8

For the pastry
250g/2 cups all-purpose (plain) flour • ½ teaspoon salt
125g/8-10 tablespoons chilled unsalted butter or margarine
1 egg, lightly beaten • 2–4 tablespoons water, or as needed

For the filling
Juice of 1 lemon • 3 large or 5 medium-sized artichokes
Olive oil • 1 large onion, diced
1 large bunch fresh flat leaf parsley, chopped (about ½ cup)
450g/1lb beet greens or spinach, coarsely chopped
350g/2 cups shelled peas • 1 tablespoon salt
½ teaspoon freshly ground black pepper • 2 eggs, lightly beaten
½ teaspoon freshly grated nutmeg, or to taste
Olive oil or lightly beaten egg for coating pastry

To make the pastry stir together the flour and salt in a bowl or in the container of a food processor.
Cut in the butter or margarine until mixture resembles coarse meal.
Add the egg and as much water as needed for the dough to come together into a rough ball.
Divide the dough in half and flatten each portion into a disk, one slightly larger than the other. Place the disks in a plastic bag and refrigerate for 1 hour.
To make the filling have ready a large bowl filled with water to which you have added the lemon juice. Working with 1 artichoke at a time, remove the stems and all the leaves until you reach the pale green heart. Pare away the dark green areas from the base.

Joyce Goldstein

Cut the artichoke in half lengthwise and scoop out and discard the choke from each half. Then cut each half into 25mm /¼-inch-thick slices and drop into the lemon water to prevent discolouration.

Pour enough olive oil into a large sauté pan to form a film on the bottom and place over medium heat. Add the onion and parsley and sauté 3 to 4 minutes.

Drain the artichokes and add to the pan along with the greens and peas. Cover and cook slowly, over low heat until the mixture is almost dry, about 10 to 15 minutes. Remove from the heat, let cool, and season with the salt, pepper, and nutmeg. Mix in the eggs.

Preheat an oven to 190°C /375°F/gas 5.

On a lightly floured work surface, roll out the larger pastry disk to a 25cm /11-inch round, about 3mm /¹/₈-inch thick. Carefully transfer to a 23cm /9-inch tart pan with a removable bottom. Spoon in the filling.

Roll out the remaining pastry disk in the same way into a 24cm /10-inch round and place over the filling. Trim any excessive overhang, then turn under the pastry edges and pinch together.

Cut a few steam vents in the top crust, then brush with olive oil or beaten egg. Bake until the crust is golden, 30 to 40 minutes.

Remove from the oven and place on a rack to cool. Serve warm or at room temperature.

NOTE

If you are worried about the bottom crust becoming soggy, sprinkle a thin layer of fine, dried breadcrumbs over the pastry before adding the filling. Alternatively, bake the bottom crust blind for 15 minutes, lining it with pie weights, let cool and then add the filling.

This vegetable filling can be used in Scacchi, a matzoh pie made during Passover. Use this vegetable mixture in place of the meat filling, and vegetable broth instead of meat broth.

PÂTES FRAÎCHES AUX PETITS POIS – NOODLES WITH CREAM, PEAS, AND PARMESAN

Although spectacular when made with fresh noodles and sweet, fresh peas, this recipe is so good that I often make it with packaged pasta and frozen baby peas. The peas can be taken from the freezer and heated in the cream whilst it thickens (in which case increase your cooking time by 1 to 2 minutes).

Pasta of all shapes and sizes can be cooked, according to the manufacturer's instructions, and mixed with the cream, peas and cheese.

DAIRY /SERVES 4-6

450g/1lb fresh pasta or 300g/10oz dried pasta
250ml/1 cup double cream • 1/8 teaspoon salt
1/8 teaspoon freshly ground pepper
130g/1 cup fresh or frozen baby peas, cooked
45g/2oz Parmesan cheese, grated

Whilst the noodles are cooking (fresh pasta only takes 3-4 minutes), in a small saucepan bring the cream to a boil over medium-high heat. Season with the salt and pepper and allow to boil gently until the cream thickens enough to coat a spoon, about 30 seconds.

Gently stir in the peas and half the cheese, heat for several seconds.

When the noodles have finished cooking, drain them in a colander and rinse under hot water. Transfer them to a warm serving bowl and pour the hot cream and pea sauce over the noodles.

Serve with the remaining cheese on the side.

Richard Grausman

CARCHOF JIBEN – SYRIAN ARTICHOKE AND CHEESE CASSEROLE

Artichokes are popular in various Mediterranean countries, where they are prepared in a wide variety of ways. Among my favourites is this simple Syrian-Jewish dish. It is a comfort food, yet also capable of serving as an appetizer at parties.

DAIRY /SERVES 6-8

3 tablespoons olive or vegetable oil • 1 large yellow onion, chopped
8 quartered artichoke bottoms or 570g/1¼lb frozen artichoke hearts, thawed
6 large eggs, lightly beaten
350g/3 cups grated Muenster, Monterey Jack,
Cheddar cheese or any combination
About 1 teaspoon salt • Ground black pepper to taste

Preheat the oven to 180°C/350°F/gas 4.

Grease a shallow 2-litre/2-quart casserole.

In a large saucepan or skillet, heat the oil over medium heat. Add the onion and sauté until soft and translucent (5 to 10 minutes). Add the artichokes and sauté until nearly tender (about 10 minutes). Remove from the heat.

Combine the eggs, cheese, salt, and pepper. Stir in the artichokes.

Spoon into the prepared casserole. Bake until golden brown (35 to 40 minutes).

VARIATIONS

Reduce the eggs to 3. Combine 145g/1 cup all-purpose (plain) flour and 1 teaspoon baking powder, then stir in 240ml /1 cup milk. Stir into the egg-cheese mixture. Add 1 teaspoon dried oregano and pinch of red pepper. Substitute 570g/1¼lb frozen chopped broccoli or spinach, thawed and drained, for the artichokes.

Gil Marks

BAKED SPINACH WITH EGGS AND CHEESE

This *tian d'épinards* is a speciality of the Vaucluse in the South of France. I have a great affection for this part of France and its cuisine since some of my art school friends bought houses in Lacoste. When Ans Hey, a Dutch sculptress, built a house on a hill in the early 1970s and her friends came to help, I put up a tent with my children and cooked for those who were building. It was mostly grills on a wood fire with substantial salads and plenty of bread. I discovered this homely bake at the local café-restaurant.

DAIRY / SERVES 4

400g/14oz fresh or frozen spinach • ½ onion, chopped
2 tablespoons butter • 2 tablespoons flour • 300ml/1¼ cups boiling milk
2 eggs, lightly beaten • Salt and pepper • Pinch of nutmeg
2 hard-boiled eggs cut into pieces • 50g/2½oz grated Gruyère

Heat the oven to 200°C/400°F/gas 6.

If using fresh spinach, wash and drain. Only remove stems if they are hard. Cook the leaves in a pan with the lid on and no added water (they steam in the water that clings to them) until they crumple. Drain in a colander and keep the juice. If using frozen whole leaf spinach, defrost, press the excess water out.

In a pan, fry the onion on low heat in the butter until soft. Add the flour and stir. Then stir in the milk and the spinach juice and cook for 5 minutes, stirring constantly to prevent lumps forming.

Add salt, pepper and nutmeg, the lightly beaten eggs, and the spinach and beat well.

Fold in the hard-boiled eggs and the Gruyère and pour into a greased 23cm/9 inch baking dish. Bake for 40 minutes or until slightly firm and golden on top.

Claudia Roden

ALIJA – VEGETABLE STEW

Alija is a deceptively tasty vegetable stew which I learned to make after watching my mother prepare this traditional Ethiopian and Eritrean dish. I grew up in a small village in Sudan and as a baby, I would have eaten Alija since there are no spices in the stew.

Alija is often eaten with *zigni*, a meat stew which is hot and spicy. Everyone shares one big plate and eats by tearing off pieces of injera – a type of fermented bread that looks a bit like a pancake – and scooping up the stews.

PARVE /SERVES 5

500g/1lb onions, medium sliced • 500g/1lb cabbage, medium sliced
750g/1½lb carrots, medium sliced • 750g/1½lb potatoes, thinly sliced
Garlic, crushed to taste • Salt and pepper to taste

Heat a little oil in a saucepan.

Fry the onions until yellow and slightly soft. Add the cabbage, fry for 10-15 minutes, stirring occasionally.

Add the carrots, potatoes, garlic and seasoning.

Cook for 30 minutes on a very low heat. You should be able to pick up the vegetables apart from the onions – they shouldn't be too soft.

Ekhlas Ahmed

SWEET-AND-SOUR STUFFED CABBAGE

My great-grandmother, Celia, born in the Ukrainian village of Prilyuki in the early 1880s, wasn't known for her cooking. But, this speciality of hers always made our mouths water. She used so much sugar that even the cabbage tasted like candy! My mother cut the sugar quantity in half when she passed down the recipe to me, and that hasn't hurt it a bit. This dish reheats beautifully. Serve with boiled potatoes or challah to mop up the sauce.

MEATY /SERVES 6

1 large green cabbage
900g/2lb minced beef • 1 egg • 100g/½ cup cooked rice
2 cans tomato paste (170g/6oz)
1 can tomato sauce (230g/8oz)
225g/1 cup sugar (Celia used 450g/2 cups—your choice)
Juice of one lemon • Salt

Cut out a little core from the bottom of the cabbage head, so the steam rises through it. Steam the cabbage head for 10-15 minutes, until the leaves are soft. Drain and cool. This step may be done ahead of time, and the leaves frozen until ready to use.

Combine the minced beef, egg and rice with 1 tablespoon of the sugar, a little tomato paste and a pinch of salt.

Place the largest, darkest cabbage leaves on the bottom of a heavy Dutch oven (deep casserole). Place a small amount of the meat mixture on a wilted cabbage leaf, roll it up and tuck in the ends. Place the rolled leaves carefully into the Dutch oven, layering the rolls on top of each other.

In a separate bowl, combine the rest of the tomato paste and sugar with the tomato sauce and lemon juice. Pour this sauce over the cabbage rolls, and add water to cover all the cabbage rolls.

Cover the Dutch oven a with lid, bring to a boil, and reduce to simmer for two hours on a very low heat. Don't let the bottom burn!

Sue Fishkoff

AUBERGINE, SWEET POTATO AND LYCHEE THAI GREEN CURRY

This vegetarian dish will certainly put a spring into spring cooking and sharpen your taste buds with its lemony overtones and subtle sweet and spicy flavours.

PARVE /SERVES 6

1 tablespoon vegetable oil • 1 tablespoon green Thai curry paste
1 onion, diced • Grated zest and juice 1 lime
2 aubergines, diced • 350g/12½oz butternut squash, diced
350g/12½oz sweet potato, diced • 425g/15oz lychees in syrup
Two sticks lemon grass • 3 lime leaves • 400ml/13½fl oz coconut milk
160ml/5½fl oz coconut cream • Pinch of salt
1 tablespoon caster sugar

Heat the oil in a wok, add the curry paste and sauté the onions until soft.

Add the lime zest, juice, aubergines, butternut squash, sweet potato, lychees, lemon grass, lime leaves, salt, coconut milk and cream. Bring to the boil and simmer for 30 minutes.

Halfway through cooking add a tablespoon of sugar, taste and if not happy, add more!

The Jewish Princesses

EGG-STUFFED CRISPY BRIK PASTRY WITH FETA, CARAMELISED SHALLOTS AND SPINACH SERVED WITH DATE SYRUP AND A HERB SALAD

The original brik dish was created by my Syrian mother, a wonderful chef who would serve it to our family for brunch accompanied by grated tomato and zchug, a cardamom and coriander sauce. I have added some feta saltiness, shallot sweetness and date syrup tanginess.

DAIRY /SERVES 4

Brik
2 large shallots, thinly sliced • 500g/2 cups baby spinach, washed
2 cloves garlic, minced • 100g/½ cup feta cheese
1 tablespoon fresh lemon thyme, chopped
(or regular thyme plus 1 teaspoon lemon zest)
8 round leaves brik pastry • 4 large eggs
60ml/¼ cup date syrup
(available in Turkish or kosher shops under the name Sylan)
120g/½ cup butter • 1 tablespoon vegetable oil
Maldon salt and coarse ground black pepper, to taste

Herb salad
1 handful each parsley, dill and mint • ½ red onion, thinly sliced
1 pomegranate, seeded

Salad Dressing
1 lemon, juiced • 1 tablespoon extra virgin olive oil
1 teaspoon caster sugar or honey
Maldon salt & coarse ground black pepper - to taste

Eran Tibi

Start by caramelising the shallots. Add them to a dry saucepan on a low/medium heat (no oil/butter needed) and cook for about 20-30 minutes, stirring from time to time with a wooden spoon (if they stick to the bottom pour a tablespoon or two of water and scrape the bottom of the pan) until the shallots turn to a light caramel colour.

Heat a saucepan on high until smoke begins to appear and then pour in a tablespoon of oil. Immediately add the garlic followed by the spinach. Stir briskly until it has reduced in volume by half, remove from the heat and drain on kitchen paper. Season.

Crumble the feta and mix with the thyme (or zest or both).

Melt 40g/3 tablespoons of the butter in a pan or microwave and brush some over one side of a single brik leaf. Immediately place another brik leaf on top and stick the two leaves together. Repeat 3 more times so you have 4 double sheeted briks.

When everybody is ready to eat, place a non-stick pan over a medium heat and add 20g/1 tablespoon of the butter. Place the double-layered brik on a large plate and in the centre place a quarter each of the shallots, spinach and feta creating a wall for the egg. Then break one egg in the middle, fold brik in half and quickly transfer to the pan. With the help of a spatula or a wooden spoon push the edges together so it seals properly. Fry for 2-3 minutes on each side until golden brown.

Remove from the pan onto kitchen paper and repeat with the rest of the briks.

Toss the herb salad with the dressing ingredients.

To serve drizzle 1 tablespoon of date syrup over the brik and top with the herb salad. A spicy and salty bloody Mary makes a great accompaniment.

DESSERTS

APPLE STRUDEL

The Gefiltefest Cookbook brings together some of the world's finest and best-loved Jewish cooks. The publishers, John Davies and Anne Dolamore, agreed to indulge me (Michael Leventhal, founder of Gefiltefest) and include one lesser-known cook: my late Grandma Sophie.

For many years no Shabbat was complete without two rolls of her perfect, freshly-made apple strudel. They were eagerly awaited and arrived every Friday afternoon, in a plastic box and were devoured by Sunday morning. She insisted we eat everything quickly whilst the pastry was fresh. The same crooked plastic box was returned so that it could be refilled the following week.

My Grandma continued to make the strudel even when she was well into her nineties. She would have been flattered – but mostly bemused and surprised to see her recipe published alongside so many renowned cooks. Regardless, it is my favourite recipe. (Picture on page 123)

PARVE /SERVES 8-10

375g/14oz ready-rolled puff pastry • Flour for dusting
1 tablespoon vegetable oil • 8 tablespoons raspberry conserve
4 tablespoons ground almonds • 4 medium Bramley (cooking) apples
170g/6oz/¾ cup raisins or sultanas • ½ teaspoon ground cinnamon
1 tablespoon beaten egg • Icing sugar, for dusting

Preheat the oven to 180°C/350°F/gas 4. Cut the sheet of pastry in half widthways.

On a lightly floured surface or a large piece of baking paper, roll one half out into a 30 x 40cm/ 11 x 15-inch rectangle – the pastry will get very thin. Lightly brush the pastry with half the oil, leaving a 2.5cm /1-inch border. Using a palette knife spread 4 tablespoons of the conserve within the border and sprinkle 2 tablespoons of the ground almonds over the top.

Peel and grate the apples into a colander, then squeeze out as much juice as you can. Spread half over the pastry, making sure the apple is evenly spread, followed by half the raisins or sultanas and a sprinkling of cinnamon.

Carefully roll from the long edge of the pastry to form a log. Turn so the seal is underneath, then tuck the ends under and brush all over with the beaten egg.

Transfer to a lined baking sheet, then repeat with the remaining pastry and ingredients.

Bake in the oven for 30-35 minutes until golden and puffed up. Leave to cool on a wire rack. When cold, sprinkle with some icing sugar, and then cut into slices. Eat and enjoy!

Grandma Sophie's

TUNISIAN FESTIVE CAKES

These recipes remind me of all the magical times I had at family weddings as well as at my own wedding!

In the Sephardic Tunisian tradition, before the bride goes to the Mikvah, all the women in her family and her friends accompany her to the Hammam. She is washed, scrubbed, perfumed, and creamed by all the members of her family and her good friends. The family prepares sweets, pastries and cakes, usually covered with honey, to wish the bride a very sweet life.

YOYO – TUNISIAN DOUGHNUTS WITH HONEY

PARVE /MAKES 12 YOYOS

25g/1oz caster sugar • 1 teaspoon vanilla sugar
1 egg • 3 tablespoons sunflower oil • 150g/¾ cup self raising flour
Oil for deep frying • 150g/¾ cup liquid honey, for the coating

Place the sugars and the egg in a bowl.

Beat well and add the oil.

Add the flour little by little mixing with your hands if possible. The dough must be soft but not sticky.

Flatten the dough with a rolling pin; it should be 1cm/½ inch thick.

With a small round cutter form some circles and make a small hole in the middle.

Deep fry the yoyos and drain them on kitchen towel to absorb the oil.

Warm the honey in a pan and dip the yoyos in it.

Eat warm or at room temperature.

Fabienne Viner-Luzzato

CORNES DE GAZELLE BISCUITS FILLED WITH MARZIPAN

PARVE /MAKES 40 CAKES

Pastry

1 egg • 5 tablespoons white wine plus a few drops
50g/¼ cup caster sugar • ½ teaspoon baking powder
25ml vegetable oil • Approximately 300g/1¼ cups plain flour
Icing sugar to dust the biscuits

Marzipan

500g/1lb ground almonds • 250g/8oz icing sugar
Few drops almond extract or rose extract
3 egg whites (you can use pasteurised egg whites for safety)

To make the pastry, mix all the ingredients together in a bowl except the flour.

Beat well, add the flour gradually in stages, and knead the dough until you obtain a non-sticky smooth dough.

To make the marzipan, put all the ingredients in a large bowl and mix well to obtain a smooth dough.

Divide the marzipan into 30 equal-sized balls and roll into small cylinder shapes.

Roll the pastry very thinly onto a floured surface.

Using a small glass or a round cutter of 5cm/2-inch diameter, cut out circles of pastry.

Put a cylinder of marzipan in the middle of each circle.

Cover the marzipan with the dough and seal the two sides of the circle together with a bit of wine, to form a little horn shape or half-moon shape biscuit.

Remove the excess dough with a pastry crimper.

Line a baking tray with some baking parchment.

Cook in a preheated oven at 160°C/325°F/gas 3 for 10 minutes.

Let them cool down and dip them in icing sugar before serving.

Fabienne Viner-Luzzato

APPLE AND APRICOT COMPOTE

DAIRY OR PARVE /SERVES 4

75g/3oz dried apricots
6-8 apples (for instance Bramley, Cox or Granny Smith)
2 teaspoons lemon juice • 50g/2oz granulated sugar
1 teaspoon pure vanilla extract • ¼ teaspoon ground cinnamon
3 tablespoons peeled and finely chopped almonds
4 tablespoons melted butter or margarine

Soak the apricots in water for 1 hour.

Preheat the oven to 180°C /350°F/gas 4. Drain the apricots and roughly chop them.

Peel the apples, cut them into quarters and remove the core. Cut the apples into thickish slices. Gently mix them in a bowl with 1 tablespoon of sugar and the lemon juice.

Grease a baking dish and place a layer of apple slices in it. Now place a layer of apricots and then another layer of apples. Continue alternately until you have used up all the apples and apricots.

Mix the remaining sugar with the cinnamon and chopped almonds. Sprinkle the mixture on top of the apples/apricots. Pour the melted butter or margarine over the whole dish.

Bake the apple apricot compote on the centre shelf of the oven for 30 minutes, by which time it will be soft and the topping golden brown. Keep an eye on it while it is baking; if the topping gets too dark, cover with a piece of aluminium foil.

NOTE

Serve this as a side dish with the Stew of Lamb and Honey (see page 77) or as a dessert.

Nanny ten Brink-de Lieme

VANILLA CHEESECAKE WITH CARAMEL PECANS AND A BUTTERSCOTCH SAUCE

This is my take on a classic baked cheesecake with some extra special topping. It takes me back to my Grandma's German cheesecake, made once a year for Shavuot when it is customary to eat dairy food, which we always looked forward to eating. I love the jewel-like broken caramel on top of this cake, and it gives a nice crunch too. If you love toffee sauce, double the quantities and keep a little jar in the fridge to heat as a sauce with ice cream and desserts.

DAIRY /SERVES 10-14

Base
250g/9oz digestive biscuits • 100g/3½oz melted butter

Filling
600g/2½ cups low fat cream cheese • 200g/7oz caster sugar
1 teaspoon vanilla extract • 300g/10oz soured cream
25g/1oz flour • 4 eggs

Pecan topping
200g/1 cup pecan nuts • 120g/4oz caster sugar

Butterscotch sauce
40g/1½oz butter • 50g/2oz soft brown sugar
40g/1½oz caster sugar • 225g/1 cup golden syrup
5 tablespoons double cream • ½ teaspoon vanilla extract

Rachel Davies

Preheat the oven to 140°C /275°F/gas 1.

Start by greasing and lining a 25cm/10 inch spring-form cake tin with baking paper. For the base, crush the biscuits with a rolling pin or in a food processor and melt the butter in a saucepan. Mix butter and biscuits together and press into the tin evenly using the back of a spoon.

For the filling, beat the cream cheese, sugar, vanilla extract, soured cream and flour together until smooth. Then whisk the eggs in, one at a time, until well combined.

Fill the cake tin with the mixture, place on a tray and bake for 60-80 minutes, or until the cheesecake is just set and lightly puffed up and golden at the sides.

Leave to cool in the tin.

For the caramel pecans, scatter the pecans on a lined baking tray and toast in the oven for 8-10 minutes. Keep an eye on them as they can burn easily.

For the caramel, put the sugar in a saucepan with enough water to just cover it. Heat gently until dissolved, and then turn the heat up to a simmer. Do not stir, but swirl occasionally to ensure that the sugar is cooking evenly. Be careful! Sugar reaches temperatures of 160°C /320°F and can cause very bad burns.

When the sugar is caramel coloured, turn off the heat, add the pecans carefully, stir until they are coated and pour onto a lined baking tray to cool. Do not touch the nuts. When they have cooled, break into chunks or chop roughly.

To make the butterscotch sauce put the butter, sugars and golden syrup into a small saucepan and bring to a gentle boil. Stir and bubble lightly for 5 minutes.

Add the cream and vanilla extract, boil for another minute, and turn off the heat and allow to cool slightly.

To finish the cheesecake, pour the slightly warmed sauce over the cheesecake and scatter the nuts over the top. Keep the cheesecake in the fridge until you want to eat it.

FRUIT COMPOTE STEEPED IN TEA

This is a simple dessert, perfect after an elaborate dinner. Cookies, slices of pound cake or even macarons could accompany the fruit, as could glasses of tawny port or snifters of brandy. The cream could be eliminated if the compote is to be served at the end of a kosher meat meal.

The whiff of bergamot in Earl Grey tea gives the drink both perfume and complexity. It does wonders for a simple compote, made by simmering dried fruit in the tea. Be sure to purchase the best quality dried fruit you can find. Which fruits to choose is up to you.

DAIRY /SERVES 8

1.3kg/3lb mixed dried fruit such as figs, prunes, apricots, peaches, cherries
2 litres/8 cups brewed Earl Grey tea
Zest of 1 orange in strips 1cm/½-inch wide
160ml/½ cup light honey • 80ml/¼ cup brandy
2 cinnamon sticks • 8 whole cloves
125ml/½ cup double cream, softly whipped, or
250ml/1 cup of crème fraîche, for serving

Combine all ingredients except the cream in a heavy saucepan. Simmer very gently for 35 minutes, until fruit is tender. You may have to add a little water during the cooking if too much of the liquid evaporates.

Allow to cool to room temperature in the pan. Chill before serving, topping each portion with a dollop of whipped cream or crème fraîche.

Florence Fabricant

LEKACH HONEY CAKE

Few cakes have a closer identification or longer history with Yiddish culture than lekach, honey cake. For centuries, no celebration or special occasion was complete without it. This recipe recalls life in Eastern Europe, where white rye flour was the best available to all but the very wealthy. Rye flour was typically eaten after the siyum on erev Pesach and on Shavuot.

PARVE /MAKES TWO LOAVES

150g/¾ cup brown sugar, packed • 1 teaspoon table salt
80ml/¹/3 cup beaten egg • 80ml/¹/3 cup vegetable oil
320ml/1¹/3 cups dark honey, preferably buckwheat
½ teaspoon ground cinnamon • ½ teaspoon ground cloves
½ teaspoon ground allspice • 160ml/²/3 cup water
1½ teaspoons baking soda • 340g/3 cups white rye flour
200-400g/1-2 cups whole or sliced nuts and/or glacé fruit (optional)

Preheat the oven to 110°C/225°F/gas ¼, with the shelf in the middle of the oven. Grease and flour or line with parchment two 22 x 12cm/8½ x 4½-inch loaf tins (pans).

In the bowl of a mixer, combine the brown sugar, salt, egg, oil, honey and spices and mix, using the flat (paddle) beater at low-medium (KA 4) speed until well blended, 6-7 minutes. Add the water and baking soda and continue mixing until blended.

Sift the rye flour and add it in 3-4 portions, blending each addition into the batter before adding the next. Continue beating for about 10 minutes. The batter will be loose, stringy and very, very sticky.

Pour the batter into the prepared loaf pans, top with sliced nuts, if desired, and bake 2 to 2½ hours.

Remove to a rack and let cool for 10-15 minutes before taking the cakes out of the pan.

NOTE

If dark honey isn't available, you may substitute 40g/1½oz of unsulphured molasses for the same quantity of honey.

Since rye and honey both attract moisture, this cake resists drying out and actually is much better after 2-3 days (if it lasts that long), especially the top crust, which turns into a soft, gooey layer of honey cream.

Stan Ginsberg

NOODLE KUGEL
WITH CHEESE AND CHERRIES

Noodle kugel is a popular parve dish, but this dairy variation can be served at Shavuot. Is it a dessert, a main or side dish? Discuss on one side of a Talmudic dissertation paper.

The recipe uses beaten egg whites for a bit of extra lightness. The latter, of course, is a relative concept in Jewish cooking.

You may find you have to adjust the sugar level to your preferred taste, but you have to steer a course between sickly and stodgy. It's trickier than it sounds, and who wants to let good food go to waste? Come to think of it, maybe you should just order in, and practise with smaller amounts before you invite company round.

DAIRY /SERVES 8

225g/1½ cups medium broad, flat egg noodles • 500g/3 cups curd cheese
250ml/1 cup soured cream • 2 heaped tablespoons sugar
4 large eggs, separated
100g/½ cup unsalted butter, melted plus extra butter for greasing
100g/½ cup dried cherries (or cranberries or raisins)
100g/½ cup toasted flaked almonds • Pinch of salt
2 teaspoons vanilla extract • 2 teaspoons ground cinnamon
½ teaspoon nutmeg, grated • Zest of 1 large lemon

Preheat the oven to 180°C/350°F/gas 4.

Cook the noodles, drain and shake them around or separate with your fingers to ensure they don't stick together in lumpy clumps, and set aside.

In a large bowl, beat together the cheese, soured cream, melted butter and the sugar. Add the egg yolks, one at a time, then stir in a pinch of salt, the cherries, almonds, spices and zest.

Stir in the noodles, cover and refrigerate for an hour.

Whip the egg whites until they are stiff and fold into the noodles. Pour into a liberally buttered, large baking dish. Bake for about 50 minutes.

If you have an old oven like mine, and the kugel starts to become burnt-brown at one side rather than golden-brown, turn the dish around now and then.

Clarissa Hyman

STRAWBERRY RHUBARB PIE MUFFINS WITH SHORTBREAD COOKIE STREUSEL

These huge, exciting muffins are more accurately delectable, single coffee-cakes than they are muffins. Brightened with chunks of garden-picked rhubarb and fresh, diced, plump strawberries, they are further dolled up with a halo of shortbread-cookie streusel. Huge caps, buttery cookie topping – this is a cause for a spring celebration! This recipe also makes beautiful mini gift loaves. I created this for my newest cookbook, *The Baker's Four Seasons*. Strawberries and rhubarb are quintessential spring flavours. Married together in a perfect little muffin, the flavours quite sing a spring 'song'.

DAIRY /MAKES 18 LARGE MUFFINS OR ABOUT 2 DOZEN SMALLER ONES

Shortbread Cookie Streusel
125g/1¼ cups shortbread cookie crumbs • 60g/¼ cup unsalted butter
60g/¼ cup sugar • 1 teaspoon vanilla powder (optional)

Muffin Batter
450g/2 cups white caster sugar • 170g/¾ cup unsalted butter, melted
60ml/¼ cup corn or canola oil • 4 eggs • 1 tablespoon pure vanilla extract
625g/5 cups all-purpose (plain) flour, approximately
4 teaspoons baking powder • 1 teaspoon baking soda • ½ teaspoon salt
250ml/1 cup buttermilk • 125ml/½ cup soured cream
150g/1½ cups diced rhubarb • 150g/1½ cups diced fresh strawberries

Marcy Goldman

Arrange oven rack to upper middle position.

Preheat the oven to 200°C/400°F/gas 6.

Line a baking sheet with parchment paper. Line a 12-cup muffin tin with muffin liners and generously spray it (including the top surface) with non-stick cooking spray. Place the pan on the baking sheet.

For the streusel, mix the cookie crumbs, butter, sugar and vanilla to make a coarse mixture and set aside.

For the muffins, in a large bowl blend the sugar with the butter and oil. Briskly whisk in the eggs and vanilla. Fold in the flour, baking powder, baking soda and salt, holding back 125g/1 cup of the flour. Add in the soured cream and buttermilk, and then mix in the last 125g/1 cup of flour (or a bit more, as required). The batter should be quite thick; if not, add in more flour.

Gently fold in the fruit. Using an ice-cream scoop, deposit generous amounts of batter into prepared muffin cups. Deposit a generous amount of the streusel on each muffin.

Bake for 30 minutes or until muffins spring back when gently touched with fingertips and are golden brown.

ALSATIAN RHUBARB TART

I learned this recipe from Michèle Weil, a paediatrician in Strasbourg. She makes all of her desserts from scratch and, like so many other French cooks I've met, uses lots of rhubarb in the spring. I especially love the way the French prepare it, without all the sugar we Americans add. Serve it with coffee or tea but it is also delicious with a sweet white wine or Champagne.

DAIRY / SERVES 8-10

Custard
1 tablespoon caster sugar • 2 large eggs • 125ml/½ cup double cream
¼ teaspoon vanilla

Crust
90g/6 tablespoons unsalted butter • 150g/1¼ cups plain flour
¼ teaspoon salt • 2 tablespoons caster sugar

Filling
900g/2lb rhubarb, peeled if stringy, and cut into 1.25cm/½-inch pieces
270g/1½ cups granulated sugar

To make the filling put the rhubarb and sugar in a heavy medium saucepan set over medium heat. Cook, stirring occasionally, for about 30 minutes or until the rhubarb is jam-like. This can be done a day ahead.

To make the crust, cut the butter into small pieces and toss into a food processor fitted with a steel blade along with the flour, salt and sugar. Pulse until the texture is like very coarse meal. Gradually add 3 tablespoons ice water, pulsing until the dough comes together in a ball. Shape the dough into a disk, cover with plastic wrap, and refrigerate for at least 45 minutes.

Preheat the oven to 190°C/375°F/gas 5 and roll out the dough. Carefully fit it into a 23cm/9-inch tart tin (pan) with a removable bottom or make it freeform on a cookie sheet. Prick it all over with a fork, and bake for 15 minutes. Remove from the oven and cool slightly.

In the meantime, beat the eggs in a small bowl. Whisk in the cream, the vanilla, and the sugar. Spread the rhubarb on the bottom of the tart. Pour the custard over the rhubarb, and bake for about 25 minutes or until golden brown and set. Serve warm or at room temperature.

Joan Nathan

STRAWBERRY-RHUBARB PIE

Rhubarb, a native of Siberia, was first eaten in Europe in the 18th century. It was introduced to America by Benjamin Franklin in 1770 during his stint as ambassador to England. Rhubarb was once such a popular American pie filling it was called 'pie plant'. In 1947, the U.S. Customs Court in Buffalo, NY, decided that rhubarb, 'whilst being a vegetable, would be forever known as a fruit, because it was eaten as a dessert more often than not'. This is my favourite springtime dessert, as the tartness of the rhubarb perfectly complements the sweetness of the berries.

DAIRY /MAKES A 23CM/9-INCH PIE OR 8 SERVINGS

Flaky pastry (pâte brisée)
280g/10oz/2 cups plain flour or pastry flour, measured by dip-and-sweep
1 tablespoon granulated sugar • 1 teaspoon salt
170g/6 oz/¾ cup shortening or butter, chilled
Approximately 80ml/¹/3 cup icy water or 5 tablespoons water mixed with
2 teaspoons cider vinegar or lemon juice

Filling
Approximately 250g/8³/₄oz/1¼ cups granulated sugar
60ml/¼ cup quick-cooking tapioca or
60ml/¼ cup cornstarch or potato starch
¼ teaspoon salt • 450g/3 cups halved strawberries
680g/3 cups fresh or 450g/16oz frozen and thawed rhubarb, cut into
1.25cm/½-inch pieces • 2 tablespoons unsalted butter or margarine

Gil Marks

To make the pastry mix the flour, sugar, and salt. Using the tips of your fingers, a pastry blender, or knives in scissors fashion, cut in the shortening until the mixture reaches a consistency of coarse crumbs.

Sprinkle icy water, 1 tablespoon at a time, over a section of the flour. Gently mix with a fork after each addition, moistening that section. Push the moistened dough aside and continue adding enough water until all the flour is barely moistened and produces a dough that holds together. Do not over mix.

Shape one third of the dough into a ball, cover with plastic wrap and flatten into a disc. Repeat with the other two thirds of the dough. Refrigerate both discs for at least 30 minutes and up to 3 days. Let stand at room temperature for about 10 minutes to soften.

Position a rack in the lower third of the oven. Preheat the oven to 220°C/425°F/gas 7.

On a lightly floured flat surface, roll out the larger disc of dough into a 30cm/12-inch round about 0.30cm/^{1}/$_8$-inch thick. Fold into half or quarters and fit into a 23cm/9-inch pie pan. Gently press into the pan. Trim the excess dough against the rim of the pan. Refrigerate.

To make the filling, combine the sugar, tapioca, and salt in a medium bowl. Stir in the strawberries and rhubarb and let stand for 15 minutes. Spoon the rhubarb mixture into the pie crust. Dot with butter.

On a lightly floured surface, roll out the smaller disc into about a 25cm/10-inch round. Cut into 1.25cm/½-inch wide strips. Weave into a lattice pattern over the filling.

Bake for 20 minutes. Reduce the heat to 180°C/350°F/gas 4 and bake until bubbles in the syrup do not burst and the pastry is golden brown (approximately 40 minutes). Place on a wire rack and let cool. If desired serve with sweetened whipped cream or vanilla ice cream.

VARIATION: CRUMBLE TOPPING

Omit the lattice topping. Combine 60g/½ cup plain flour, 110g/½ cup granulated sugar, 30g/¼ cup rolled oats, and ½ teaspoon ground cinnamon. Then, cut in 30g/¼ cup softened butter or margarine until crumbly. Sprinkle over the top of the unbaked pie.

HAZELNUT CAKE WITH CHOCOLATE GANACHE

Growing up in South Africa and long before carrot cakes were in vogue, my mother 'invented' this wonderfully moist cake. For a rich dessert, I top the cake with a dark chocolate ganache. My mum used a thin rum icing drizzled over the top which is also delicious and not as rich.

DAIRY /SERVES 12

Cake
5 eggs, separated • 90g/6 heaped tablespoons caster sugar
250g/8oz ground hazelnuts (finely ground but not to a paste)
1 large carrot, peeled and finely grated • Pinch salt
½ teaspoon cream of tartar

Icing
250g/10oz dark chocolate • 250g/10oz double cream

Preheat the oven to 180°C /350°F /gas 4.

Grease and paper the base of a 25cm /10-inch spring form tin. There is no need to grease the sides of the tin.

Beat the egg yolks with the sugar and salt until snow white.

Fold in the hazelnuts.

Fold in the grated carrot.

Beat the egg whites until foamy, add the cream of tartar and beat until stiff.

Gently fold the stiffly beaten egg whites into the egg yolk mixture.

Pour into the tin, heaping the mixture in the centre.

Bake for 40 minutes or until light golden brown and a skewer comes out clean. The cake should spring back when touched.

Remove from the oven and allow to cool completely before icing.

Bring the cream to scorching point (just before boiling point is reached).

Pour it over the broken chocolate in a glass bowl and whisk until fully blended, smooth and shiny.

Use the icing once it is starting to thicken and set. Spread thickly over the top of the cake.

Rosalind Rathouse

RUGELACH THREE WAYS

The first rugelach I tasted was baked by my grandma Sylvia from Brooklyn to whom I dedicated my first cookbook. Her version was a flaky dough filled with nuts and raisins and covered with powdered sugar.

Now I prefer rugelach dough made with cream cheese, which I easily converted to parve with soy cream cheese. Here are three fillings to choose from. If you prefer to make one type, double one of the filling recipes (each filling amount is enough for half the dough). You can also use coconut, raisins, currants, chopped nuts or jam as fillings to make your own signature cookie.

PARVE /MAKES 50-60 PIECES

225g/1 cup parve margarine • 230g/1 cup parve cream cheese, softened
265g/2 cups plus 2 tablespoons all-purpose (plain) flour,
plus extra for rolling out dough
1 tablespoon confectioners' (icing) sugar

Chocolate Filling
112g/¾ cup parve chocolate chips • 6 tablespoons parve whipping cream
30g/¼ cup pecan halves (optional)

Apricot and Cinnamon Filling
165g/½ cup apricot jam or preserve • 2 tablespoons sugar
1 teaspoon ground cinnamon

Orange and Pine Nut Filling
165g/½ cup sweet orange marmalade • 45g/¹/3 cup pine nuts

To make the dough, place the margarine, cream cheese, flour, and confectioners' sugar in the bowl of a mixer or food processor fitted with a metal blade and mix just until dough comes together.

Divide the dough in half and wrap each ball in plastic and flatten. Freeze for 1½ hours or refrigerate overnight and then freeze ½ hour before using. The dough is ready to be rolled when you can press gently into it. If it gets too soft, put it back in the freezer to firm up.

Preheat the oven to 180°C /350°F/gas 4.

Paula Shoyer

To roll out the rugelach, place a large sheet of parchment on the counter. Sprinkle some flour on the parchment, place one of the dough discs on the parchment, sprinkle again with flour, and then top with a second sheet of parchment. Rolling on top of the parchment, roll out the dough to 25 x 38cm/ 10 x 15 inches. Peel back the top parchment once or twice whilst rolling and sprinkle some more flour on the dough. Remove the top parchment but reserve for re-use. This portion of dough is now ready to be filled with one of the three fillings, or another filling of your choice.

After filling the dough, fold the right and left sides (the short sides) of the dough 1.25cm/½ inch towards the centre to keep the filling inside. Using the parchment to help you, roll the long side from the top towards you, working slowly and rolling up as tightly as you can, like a swiss roll or roulade.

Place the parchment [which you used on top of the dough when rolling it] to line a cookie sheet. Place the roll on the cookie sheet with the join underneath and flatten slightly.

Bake for 35 to 40 minutes, or until the top begins to brown. Let cool and then slice into 1 inch/2.5cm pieces. These can be frozen. I prefer to freeze the baked loaves and then slice them when ready to serve.

CHOCOLATE FILLING

Melt the chocolate chips on the hob or in the microwave in 30 second increments, mixing often until the chocolate is smooth.

Remove from heat and add cream.

If using the pecans place the pecan halves in a plastic bag and crush with a rolling pin.

Spread the chocolate mixture evenly on the dough all the way to the edges and then sprinkle with pecan pieces.

APRICOT AND CINNAMON FILLING

Spread the apricot jam or preserve evenly on the dough.

Combine sugar and cinnamon in a small bowl and then sprinkle on top of the jam.

ORANGE AND PINE NUT FILLING

Spread the orange marmalade over the dough and sprinkle on the pine nuts.

ORANGE AND ANISE GLAZED SWEET POTATO SFINGE, STEWED BLACK GRAPES AND GREEK YOGHURT

'Sfinge' or Moroccan doughnuts are typical Chanucah treats. They are quite easy to prepare. The best thing is that you can't overcook the potatoes or over fry them since the more you brown them in the oil the crunchier they become. The only difficult thing is that they do not always turn out as ring-shaped cakes as they traditionally should be. Crispy with a sticky glaze and rather unusually served with juicy black grapes and creamy yoghurt. Say no more, it's a mouth-watering delight!

DAIRY/SERVES 4

Sfinge
250g/1 cup potatoes, peeled, cubed evenly and boiled
(I use 150g sweet potatoes and 100g any starchy potatoes)
350g/1½ cups self-raising flour • 20g/4 teaspoons salt
25g/1oz/1 tablespoon sugar • 40g/¼ cup baking powder
2 oranges, zest of one and juice of both • 220ml/7oz full fat milk
Oil for frying

For the grapes
400g/1¾ cups black seedless grapes on their stalks
30g/¼ cup brown sugar • 1 lemon, juiced • 2 tablespoons water

For the glaze
50g/¼ cup sugar • 50ml/¼ cup water
3 star anise • 1 orange, zest only • Juice from stewed grapes
Yoghurt, for serving • Flaked almonds, for serving

Eran Tibi

Crush the potatoes with a fork and add all the dry ingredients. Then add all the wet ingredients (orange juice, zest and milk), knead together and 'beat' the pastry repeatedly with your hands to make a thick batter (you can use a pastry spatula or a wooden spoon if you don't want to get messy). You should end up with a sticky and wet dough. Let it rest for one hour in a cool area but not in the fridge.

Preheat the oven to 220°C /425°F/gas 7.

Gently – so the grapes stay on their stalks – toss all the ingredients for the grapes in a bowl and place on an oven proof tray lined with baking paper. Roast for roughly 5-7minutes.The grapes should soften and burst just a bit, yet not be too mushy as they continue cooking as they cool down.

Place all the ingredients for the glaze in a saucepan (including the juices from the stewed grapes). Cook it down for 10-15 minutes on a low heat until it coats the back of a wooden spoon.

Heat oil in a large saucepan until a small amount of batter dropped in the oil sizzles and starts to colour. With a teaspoon (dip the teaspoon in the oil so it's easier to scoop for a more impressive presentation) drop one pound coin size balls into the oil.

Deep-fry until dark brown and crunchy on both sides. Remove with a slotted spoon and drain on kitchen paper.

To serve: toss the doughnuts in the glaze, place in a large serving bowl and dollop with the yoghurt. Decorate with a bunch of the grapes on its stalk and finish with a sprinkle of flaked almonds.

BABKA

This braided yeast cake with chocolate and halva is a favourite in the Jewish repertoire. I add halva crumbs, a popular Middle Eastern sweet, to give the cake added texture and flavour.

DAIRY /MAKES 2 LOAVES

For the dough
560g/4½ cups all-purpose (plain) flour • 10g/3½ teaspoons dry yeast
100g/7 tablespoons sugar • 100g/7 tablespoons softened butter
2 eggs • 180ml/¾ cup milk
1 teaspoon salt • 1 teaspoon vanilla extract

Filling
Chocolate spread • Halva crumbs

Coating
1 egg, lightly beaten

Put all the dough ingredients in a large mixing bowl and knead by hand or in a stand mixer until a smooth and flexible dough is formed.

Cover loosely with a tea towel and allow to rise until doubled in volume.

On a lightly floured surface, roll out the dough into a large rectangle about 1cm /½-inch thick.

Cover the dough with the chocolate spread and sprinkle generously with halva crumbs.

Roll up lengthwise into a tight log and press down slightly to seal. Cut the log in half.

Slice one of the log halves in half lengthwise down the middle and loosely twist together to form a braid. Repeat with the remaining dough log.

Transfer each braid to a parchment-lined loaf pan and brush with egg. Set aside and allow to rise for another 15 minutes.

Meanwhile heat the oven to 170°C/340°F/gas 3.

Bake the babka for about 10 minutes until golden. Allow to cool slightly before slicing.

SYRIAN APRICOT COMPOTE IN ROSEWATER SYRUP

Apricots originally grew in China thousands of years ago. Today most of our fresh apricots come from California, and the large, prized, dried apricots come from Turkey and Syria. Because apricots bruise easily, their farm to market popularity peaks in June and July. Good-quality dried apricots, however, can be purchased year-round, so I have adapted a classic Middle Eastern recipe to use the dried variety.

PARVE /SERVES 4

175g/6oz dried apricots • 500ml/2 cups water
225g/1 cup sugar • 30g/¼ cup slivered almonds
60g/½ cup pistachios • ½ teaspoon rose water

Combine apricots with water in a microwavable bowl. Microwave on high for 2 minutes, and let the apricots sit in the water, covered, for 2 hours or overnight.

When apricots are soft, drain them, reserving the soaking water.

Measure 125ml/½ cup of soaking water and place in a clean glass bowl. Add the sugar, and microwave on high for 1 minute or until sugar is dissolved. Set aside to cool.

Toast slivered almonds in a 160°C/ 325°F/gas 3 oven for 4 minutes or until lightly golden and fragrant.

Return the apricots to the bowl. Add the pistachios, toasted almonds, and rose water to the bowl. Stir to combine and chill until ready to serve.

NOTE

This mixture is traditionally eaten without accompaniment in shallow dishes but may be served over vanilla ice cream, yoghurt, or sponge cake for a more Western dessert.

Microwaving dried foods submerged in water for 2 or 3 minutes allows them to hydrate significantly faster than letting them soak at room temperature for 5 hours or overnight. Although the kernel of the apricot pit is used, after roasting, for flavouring sweets and liqueurs, in its raw state the pit is poisonous and should not be used.

Tina Wasserman

LIBBY SKLAMBERG'S PASSOVER SPONGE CAKE

Sponge cake, or *lekach* as it's known in Yiddish, is the quintessential Yiddish snack food, so much so that the phrase *lekach un bronfn*, 'sponge cake with whisky,' has come to mean any reception at which you get a free shot of booze and something solid to go with it.

I got this recipe from my late friend, Libby Sklamberg; I was originally a friend of her son, Lorin, lead singer of the Klezmatics, but Libby and I quickly bonded over a shared love of old Hollywood movies. This isn't the only recipe that she sent me, but it's definitely my favourite.

PARVE /MAKES 6–8 HEALTHY SLICES

9 large eggs (separate 7) • 150g/¾ cup sugar
80ml/¹⁄₃ cup orange juice • 1 tablespoon orange zest
1 teaspoon lemon juice (optional) • ½ teaspoon lemon zest (optional)
2 heaping tablespoons potato starch
250g/1 cup minus 2 heaping tablespoons matzo cake meal

Place oven rack on lowest level.

Preheat the oven to 180°C/350°F/gas 4.

In a metal bowl, beat 7 egg whites until they are stiff and set them aside.

In a second bowl, beat 7 egg yolks plus 2 whole eggs. Gradually add the sugar, continuing to beat the mixture until it is pale yellow.

Add the orange juice and zest (plus lemon juice and zest, if desired).

With your mixer at its lowest speed, add the potato starch and matzo cake meal to the yolk mixture.

Remove the bowl from the mixer stand.

Put the bowl with the egg whites on the mixer stand. Again, using the lowest speed, pour half of the yolk mixture slowly into the whites. Fold in the remaining yolk mixture.

Pour into an ungreased tube tin (pan) with a removable bottom.

Bake and check the cake after 55 minutes. Do not open the oven door before that, or your cake will fall. The sponge cake should be golden brown and spring back to the touch.

Difficult as it might be to believe, two slices of this cake provide the foundation for a superb kosher-for-Passover egg-salad sandwich. It not only solves the vexed soggy-matzoh problem, but also turns a rather humdrum sandwich into a main course that tastes like dessert.

Michael Wex

ACKNOWLEDGEMENTS

We would not have been able to complete this first cookbook without the support of an unseen army of volunteers who tested each recipe. Over the last two years Naomi Capper and Lainie Dropkin have worked tirelessly, editing and proofreading the manuscript. Anne Dolamore and John Davies of Grub Street have also been patient, supportive and enthusiastic throughout the production of the book.

Gefiltefest relies on a team of volunteers to stage an annual Jewish food festival at the London Jewish Cultural Centre and other food-related events throughout the year. We have also received generous financial support from the Ethical Superstore, the Grove Hotel, JHub, Leket Israel, the Natan Fund and the Shoresh Charitable Trust.

It is impossible to list everyone who has attended our events, presented sessions at our four festivals, supported this cookbook and helped with our other endeavours but we are grateful to the following individuals:

Allan Bailey, Richard Baruch, Susan Baruch, Judy Berman, Betty Berson, Shoshana Boyd Gelfand, Shana Boltin, Amy Braier, Nelson Burke, Joanna Cohen, Russell Collins, Denise Connick, Natasha Cowan, Melody Dadon, Laura Dahan, Rachel Davies, Saul Doctor, Patrick Dodds, Miriam Dub-Israel, Josh Dwek, Jackie Fishman, Anthony Foreman, Richard Freeman, Rebecca Geller, Carl Gilbert, Odelia Ghrenassia, Felicia Herman, Annette Holst, Nicole Horowitz, Julian Hunt, Anna Hyman, Ronee Isaacson, Natasha Kahn, Adam Kendler, Maureen Kendler, Andrew Kennard, Alan Klein, Olivia Klevan, Tarryn Klotnick, Debby Konigsberg, Denise Lahat, Anne Larchy, Anick Landau-Leboff, Elizabeth Leventhal, Matt Leventhal, Martha Lewis, Miriam Lewis, Sandy Littman, Oliver Marcus, Rachel Marcus, Toni Marcus, Eddie Marshbaum, Arnold Moscisker, Silvia Nacamulli, Natalie Nederkoorn, Charlotte Newman, Debbie Newman, Ruth Newman, Claudia Prieto, Eliane Rahmani, Susannah Raye, Esther Roling, Michelle Rose, Paul Rosen, Simon Rosenberg, Hana Ross, Steph Saffer, Nigel Savage, Dani Serlin, Daniel Sher, Sophie Silver, Anthony Silverman, Katie Susser, Rachel Savage, Ben Sheriff, Corinne Sheriff, Daliah Sherrington, Corinne Shmuel, Karina Stevenson, Charles Taylor, Jonathan Teacher, Judy Trotter, Danielle Vides, Annie Wigman, Charlotte Whiting, Lea Yehud and Sergey Yelnik.

Gefiltefest is a fast-expanding charity and this listing was written in October 2013 – apologies to anyone who has volunteered since then and has not been included! If you are interested in volunteering for any Gefiltefest project, please check our website www.gefiltefest.org or email gefiltefest@gmail.com.

CONTRIBUTORS

NADINE ABENSUR was born in Morocco of French-Jewish parents and draws on this heritage and her many travels to create original vegetarian recipes; www.nadineabensur.com

EKHLAS AHMED grew up in a small village in Sudan and now lives in London. She is a member of Spice Caravan, a catering social enterprise and co-operative of eight women from Sudan, Somalia and Eritrea.

KEN ALBALA is an American Professor of Food History who has written about food in the Middle Ages and Early Modern Europe as well as a global history of pancakes and a textbook *Three World Cuisines: Italian, Mexican and Chinese.*

MICHAL ANSKY is a Jerusalem born culinary expert and entrepreneur, television presenter, author and food journalist. She founded the first Israeli farmers market and her first cookbook *Food from Home* was published in 2013.

TORI AVEY is a food writer and recipe writer who explores how the foods of different cultures have evolved and how yesterday's food can inspire us in the kitchen today; www.theshiksa.com and www.thehistorykitchen.com

CLAIRE BERSON is a food writer who shares her passion for soup on her website www.ilove-soup.net.

NANNY TEN BRINK-DE LIEME was born in 1930 in the Netherlands and has been writing a culinary column since 1971. She has published a cookbook *Mijn Joodse Keuken* (*My Jewish Kitchen*).

JAYNE COHEN writes and lectures on Jewish cuisine and culture and is the author of *Jewish Holiday Cooking: A Food Lover's Treasury of Classics and Improvisations.* Visit jewishholidaycooking.com

SIBEL CUNIMAN-PINTO is an Istanbul-born cook, researcher and writer specialising in Mediterranean cuisines and the author of the award winning *The Evolution of the Sephardic Cuisine in Turkey: Five Centuries of Survival.* Visit www.sibelpinto.com

LINDA DANGOOR was born in Baghdad. A professional artist and a passionate cook, she has recently written *Flavours of Babylon*, a cookery book featuring recipes of the Babylonian Jewish community.

RACHEL DAVIES is a Cordon Bleu trained chef, cookery teacher and recipe writer. She set up Rachel's Kitchen in 2010; www.rachels-kitchen.com

POOPA DWECK is an expert on the food and customs of the Jews of Aleppo in Syria and the author of *Aromas of Aleppo: The Legendary Cuisine of the Syrian Jews*.

JAMES AND MICHAEL EDER founded studentbeans.com which provides students with discounts, entertainment and advice on all things student. With the help of their website's food editor, they have created *The Ultimate Student Cookbook: Cheap, Fun, Easy, Tasty Food*.

FLORENCE FABRICANT is the food and wine columnist for the *New York Times* and author of 11 cookbooks.

SUE FISHKOFF is a San Francisco-based Jewish journalist and the author of *Kosher Nation: Why More and More of America's Food Answers to a Higher Authority*.

JAMIE GELLER is the co-founder of the Kosher Media Network and as well as her website, www.joyofkosher.com, she hosts an online television cookery show Quick and Kosher.

TAMAR GENGER is the Executive Editor with Jamie Geller of www.joyofkosher.com, the No.1 kosher food and recipe website featuring more than 6,000 recipes.

STAN GINSBERG is the co-author of *Inside the Jewish Bakery: Recipes and Memories from the Golden Age of Jewish Baking*; www.insidethejewishbakery.com

SHARON GLASS is a chef and author who has written nine bestselling cookbooks and is also a well-loved TV personality with the second series of her own show, Sharon's Simple Stylish Meals having aired earlier this year. Her passion for cooking is simply contagious. www.sharonglass.co.za.

SIMI GOLDBERG is an Israeli cook of Iraqi origin and the brainchild of Falafel Feast which caters for every type of falafel and salad combination; www.falafelfeast.co.uk

MARCY GOLDMAN is a Montreal-based pastry chef and master baker. The creator and host of the renowned baker's site, www.BetterBaking.com, her cookbooks include *A Treasury of Jewish Holiday Baking* and *The Baker's Four Seasons*.

JOYCE GOLDSTEIN is a consultant to the restaurant and food industries and a prolific cookbook author, teacher and lecturer. For twelve years, she was chef/owner of the ground-breaking Mediterranean restaurant Square One in San Francisco having previously been chef of the Cafe at Chez Panisse.

TODD GRAY and **ELLEN KASSOFF GRAY** own and operate Equinox Restaurant in Washington, D.C. Todd is a five-time James Beard Award Nominee.

RICHARD GRAUSMAN taught at Le Cordon Bleu Paris 1969-1985 earning the coveted Grand Diplôme. In 1990, he founded the Careers through Culinary Arts Program; www.ccapinc.org He is the author of *French Classics Made Easy*.

GIL HOVAV is an Israeli culinary journalist and television personality, and has published three best-selling novels and a dozen cookbooks. For the past 24 years, he has lived with his partner Danny. Together they raise their daughter, Naomi.

CLARISSA HYMAN is an award-winning food and travel writer based in the UK. She has written three books and plays an active role in the Slow Food Movement.

JUDY JACKSON has written seven cookbooks and a 'foodie' novel *The Camel Trail*. Her daily blog The Armchair Kitchen features both food and books; www.lookitcookit.tumblr.com

RUTH JOSEPH is the prize-winning co-author of *Warm Bagels and Apple Strudel* and writes a blog with her daughter Sarah; veggieschmooze.blogspot.com. Her website is ruthjoseph.co.uk

THE JEWISH PRINCESSES aka Georgie Tarn and Tracey Fine are the creators of the bestselling Jewish Princess cookbooks and brand; www.thejewishprincess.com

MICHAEL LEVENTHAL is the Director of Greenhill Books and Publisher of Frontline Books, both history book imprints. He is the co-author of *Jews in Britain* (Shire Publications, 2013). He is the founder and director of Gefiltefest, a Jewish food charity inspiring people to think differently about food.

FAYE LEVY is a long-time columnist of the *Jerusalem Post*, has lived on three continents and has written cookbooks in English, French and Hebrew including *Feast from the Mideast* and *1000 Jewish Recipes*.

SHARON LURIE'S passion for food lies solely in the fact that 'time out' is time spent in the kitchen! Married to a kosher butcher in South Africa, her latest book is *Celebrating with the Kosher Butcher's Wife*.

DEBORAH MADISON is an American chef, writer and cookery teacher. She specialises in vegetarian cooking and her work highlights Slow Food, local foods and farmers' markets.

GIL MARKS, an award-winning writer, historian, rabbi, and chef, is a leading authority on culinary subjects and Jewish cuisine. His books include *Encyclopedia of Jewish Food*, *Olive Trees and Honey*, and *The World of Jewish Cooking*.

SILVIA NACAMULLI raised in Rome but now living in London, runs her own catering company La Cucina di Silvia, www.cookingforthesoul.com. She also teaches, writes and lectures on Italian Jewish cooking.

HELEN NASH is an innovator in the field of kosher cooking who studied traditional Italian cooking under the renowned chef, Marcella Hazan. Her cookbook, *Helen Nash's New Kosher Cuisine* and her website www.helennashkoshercuisine.com is full of Italian-inspired recipes.

JOAN NATHAN is a regular contributor to *The New York Times*, *Food Arts Magazine* and *Tablet Magazine*. She has also written 10 cookbooks including *Quiches, Kugels and Couscous: My Search for Jewish Cooking in France*.

RUSSELL NORMAN is the co-founder of POLPO, Spuntino and Mishkin's. He is the author of *POLPO A Venetian Cookbook (Of Sorts)*, which has won a number of prestigious awards.

YOTAM OTTOLENGHI and **SAMI TAMIMI**, both native Jerusalemites, are the men behind the Ottolenghi chain of restaurants and the authors of *Ottolenghi: The Cookbook* and the recently published *Jerusalem*.

PHILIP PELL is the co-owner of Kaifeng, the celebrated Glatt kosher Chinese restaurant in London; www.kaifeng.co.uk

DENISE PHILLIPS is a renowned chef and food columnist and the author of 5 cookbooks. Denise has her own Jewish recipe collection on line – also available as a mobile app. Date on a Plate, her unique cookery classes for singles, is an excellent way of networking, cooking and meeting new people. www.jewishcookery.com

FRED PLOTKIN is a New Yorker with an expertise in Italian food as well as opera and author of *Italy for the Gourmet Traveler*.

VICTORIA PREVER is Food Editor of the *Jewish Chronicle*, a freelance food writer and professionally trained chef. She also teaches cookery. www.yummiestmummy.co.uk

ROSE PRINCE is the *Daily Telegraph's* food columnist and the author of five books, including *Kitchenella*, *The New English Kitchen*, and *The Savvy Shopper*.

STEVEN RAICHLEN is a multi-award-winning author, journalist, and television host. His 29 books include *The Barbecue Bible*, *How to Grill* and *The Planet Barbecue*.

ROSALIND RATHOUSE is a professional cook who founded Cookery School in central London in 2003 after having taught cookery for many years in both England and her native South Africa; www.cookeryschool.co.uk

CLAUDIA RODEN was born in Cairo and now lives in London. She is a food writer with a special interest in the cultural, social and historical background of food exemplified in *The Book of Jewish Food: An Odyssey from Samarkand and Vilna to the Present Day*. She is the founding patron of Gefiltefest.

EVELYN ROSE was an authority on food and wine who became very well known in the Anglo-Jewish community through her weekly cookery column for the *Jewish Chronicle* and her bestselling cookbooks.

ALAN ROSENTHAL created his own food brand Stewed! – a range of tasty, as good as homemade stew pots and has written a cookbook *Stewed! Nourish your Soul* containing a feast of one pot dishes. He runs cookery workshops with Leith's school of Food and Wine.

MICHAEL RUHLMAN is an American author, home cook and entrepreneur who has collaborated with Thomas Keller on cookery books as well as having written several of his own. His latest book is *The Book of Schmaltz: A Love Song to a Forgotten Fat*. ruhlman.com

LADY SACKS qualified as a radiographer at Addenbrooke's Hospital and is involved in various charities and organisations. She loves to entertain and cook for family and friends and manages to fit cooking into her very busy schedule.

NIGEL SAVAGE, an Englishman in NY, is one of the leaders of the American Jewish Food Movement, and the founder of Hazon. nigel@hazon.org /www.hazon.org

MICHAEL SHAFRAN is a professional food and wine writer based in Sydney, the author of a website called The Melting Pot and the Chief Epicurial Officer of Gosstronomy.com

LEAH SHAPIRA is an American food columnist who has recently launched a kosher recipe-sharing website; www.cookkosher.com

PAULA SHOYER is a pastry chef who owns and runs Paula's Parisian Pastries Cooking School in Maryland. She received her pastry diploma from the Ritz Escoffier Ecole de Gastronomie Française in Paris; www.paulapastry.com.

MARLENA SPIELER has been writing about food since she fell in love with cooking, over 50 books ago. She broadcasts on BBC Radio 4 and writes for a variety of publications worldwide; www.marlenaspieler.com

ERAN TIBI acquired his basic cookery skills and love of sephardi food from his parents, his Tunisian father and his Syrian mother, who run a bakery in Petah Tikva. He now lives in London where he worked at Le Cordon Blue, Ottolenghi, Made in Camden and Chef's Playground. Today Eran is one of the main chefs at Zest, the restaurant at JW3.

FABIENNE VINER-LUZZATO grew up in Paris and her cooking style and love of Mediterranean flavours are influenced by her Tunisian mother and Italian father. She is a professional caterer and cookery teacher; www.homecookingbyfabienne.co.uk

TINA WASSERMAN is the author of *Entree to Judaism*, a world renowned speaker and cookery teacher, a food columnist for *Reform Judaism* magazine and a member of Les Dames d'Escoffier.

MICHAEL WEX is the Canadian author of *Born to Kvetch*, the bestselling book ever written about Yiddish. He is also a columnist, bon vivant and raconteur; www.michaelwex.com.

PAULA WOLFERT is the author of eight cookbooks including the classic *Couscous and Other Good Food from Morocco* which she wrote whilst living in Tangier and all her books have a strong Mediterranean flavour.

ORLY ZIV is a nutritionist and cooking instructor from Tel Aviv. She is a culinary tour guide at www.cookinisrael.com. She has written several cookbooks which draw on her Jewish-Greek heritage and her recipes are full of Middle Eastern and Mediterranean flavours.

INDEX